WILL LIVE MY
POWER – PURPOSE – PLAN

BIGGER DREAMS REQUIRE BIGGER FAITH
- Kalena

KALENA FITZGERALD JAMES

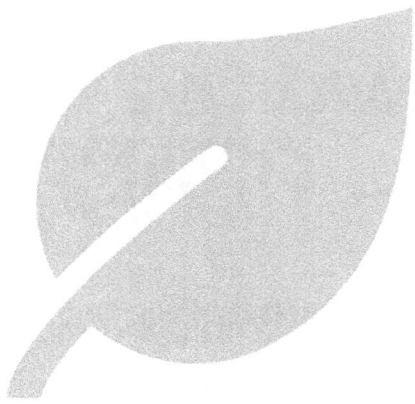

I Will Live My Power – Purpose – Plan
Copyright © 2017 by Kalena James

All rights reserved. No part of this book may be reproduced or transmitted in any form or by any means without written permission from the author.

ISBN-13: 978-0692959473
ISBN-10: 0692959475

Disclaimer: This book is a work of nonfiction. However, some of the names, persons, places, and incidents are based on the author's account or memory. Some individuals' names have been changed.

First Edition 2017
Published & Printed in the United Stated by
Beloved Daffodils Inspirations- Kokomo, Indiana 46902

DEDICATION

For Vaughn, Olivia, and Bishop

This book is dedicated to all the young girls who had to push through obstacles to find the power of their voice, the struggle of their purpose, and the determination to go for the plan God's has for you. Special thanks to Benita A. Tyler for helping me give my voice to the world. You were an answer to my prayers. To my pastors Melvin Warren of Light of Liberty Church, Cleveland Ohio and James Bradley of Family Worship Center, Kokomo Indiana. This book is also dedicated to my grandparents Owen and Jackie Fitzgerald until I see you again on the other side. Special thanks to my mother Julie Fitzgerald Lewis who did her best to raise my brothers and me, I love you so much, you were the mother I needed. To Olivia and Bishop, you are my favorite children. I'm so proud of who you are and what your life contributes to this world! You are my greatest accomplishment in life. Finally, to the man who is everything I never knew I always wanted! Vaughn, you are the love my life, and I'm so happy that I get to be your wife.

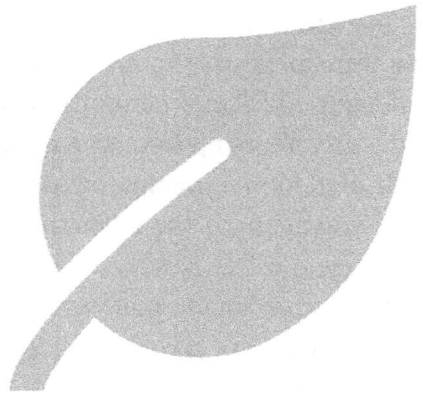

#POWERPURPOSEPLAN

Dedication 3

Acknowledgements 7

Chapter 1 Power Unleashed 9

Chapter 2 Power Discovered 41

Chapter 3 Power in Being Kalena 65

Chapter 4 Power of Being Beautiful 81

Chapter 5 Power in Finding My Daddy 101

Chapter 6 Power in Protecting My Mother 109

Chapter 7 Power of Forgiveness 123

Chapter 8 Power of Being His 138

Chapter 9 Power of Being Mrs. James 152

Chapter 10 Purpose Finding Way 170

Chapter 11 Planning Fearlessly 186

ACKNOWLEDGEMENTS

"I am the Ray that causes a deep breath that awakens the soul."

- Kalena James

"We got one shot at this race called life we might as well…LIVE it!"

Beautiful ladies of "The City of Firsts United State of Women Power Brunch," thank you for helping me to generate a movement. As I've said before, we're Diamonds, that shine bright, but when we're together we shine so much brighter!

#powerpurposeplan

CHAPTER 1

Power Unleashed

If I told you that ever since I was a little girl, I had the capacity to influence the behavior of others or the course of events would you believe me? God gives all of his children a measure of power, but its distribution isn't always equal. My thoughts, feelings, and family, all had an effect on my personal power. I had to learn to maneuver through the obstacles, you know what I'm talking about, those huge roadblocks, and relentless life lessons we all get to go through. People assume that throughout my life it has been easy for me to stand in my truth, but I'm here to tell you things weren't always that easy.

It didn't matter what I was born into I knew deep down inside that I was destined to be so much more than my circumstances. Yes! More than I or anyone could have imagined. Allow me to take you on this journey starting from my childhood to demonstrate how I learned to use my power to define the woman I am today. God has shown me time after time that He won't count me out for I am His makings of a phenomenal woman.

Fitzgerald! That's my namesake. My story begins with two of the most influential people in my life and the impact they had on me. My maternal grandparents Owen and Jackie Fitzgerald, were the backbone of our family. They lived in the Maple Heights section of Cleveland, Ohio. Their address 5590 Lafayette Avenue, will forever be etched in my mind. They lived in a yellow two-story, four-bedroom house with red shutters that would eventually be my home too.

A lot of memories were generated in that house. My grandparents were vibrant people who nurtured their two boys and three girls the best they could. My grand-dad was a distinguished gentleman who fought in World War II. From my vantage point, he always seemed so serious, but I was the one he took the time to impart his great wisdom into. My grandmother was the glue that held our family together. She was a functional alcoholic who drank every day just to get by. Boy was she stern, I imagine her children did very little to cross her. My grandparents were no different from other folks who lived in that era. My grand-dad believed a man's role was to go out into the world and make money to take care of his family, and the man's wife role was to stay home and raise their children.

My grand-dad also had another set of expectations for my grandmother. He expected her to keep the house clean and have a hot meal ready for him when he got off work. My grandmother was a good cook and every day she rose to the occasion to meet his expectations. They loved each other dearly and were married for fifty years. My grand-dad died when I was twenty-five, leaving a hole bigger than the state of Ohio in my heart. My grandmother died two years later, which I believe was from a broken heart. Suddenly, my heroes had gone to a better place. I thank God for their influence, and for the part they played in helping me to tap into my power no matter the circumstances.

My mother was the youngest daughter of their five children. My grandparents named her Julie. When she was growing up, her siblings described her as shy, but she learned how to advocate for herself later in life. She lived in their shadows and desired to find her own identity. My mother was a homebody, who was naïve about most things. She was a fair skinned black girl of average height, and slightly overweight which didn't help her self-esteem. Her feelings about her weight caused her to suppress the leader within. She stopped dreaming about a brighter future. Back then, mothers were too busy to invest in their daughters the way we do today. My mom didn't have a role model to coach, nurture, and to instill in her that all girls are beautiful in their own way. She was on her own; self-awareness escaped her but was waiting to be found.

My mother made some poor decisions as a teenager, one of which was to have sex before marriage. She also dropped out of school when she was in the eleventh grade. Shortly after dropping out, she realized that her decision to place her education on hold was something she'd come to regret later in life. Her decision had a lot to do with a handsome young man who would change her life forever. His name was Larry Hullum, a tall, handsome brown-skinned young man with big brown eyes that seemed to have the attention of a lot of girls in their neighborhood. He was a smooth-talking ladies' man who'd become my daddy. My mother fell head over heels for him, and she was willing to give up the better parts of herself to please him. Still a virgin when they met she desired to have a physically and emotionally relationship with him. If you asked some of her friends back then they'd say, "Julie was so sweet and innocent," but little did they know, she was willing to play a game of cat and mouse with Larry believing she could hold his attention.

Although my mother was shy, she had friends and examples around, including her sisters, who were sassy and attractive and knew how to attract the guys they wanted who she could emulate. They were boy crazy and spent a lot of time chasing after them. My mother believed that she needed to lose some weight to get Larry to chase her. She knew she had a pretty face, great personality, and good hair, but she wanted a brick house body to match.

My mother needed to come up with a plan. She recalled a conversation between my grandmother and one of her friends. My grandparents always had a lot of company on the weekends when my grand-dad wasn't working. Their house was always full of laughter and the smell of soul food. My grandmother prepared big feasts that consisted of fried chicken, catfish, collard greens and cornbread which quickly was demolished as soon as she sat it down on the kitchen table. They'd party in the basement into the wee hours of the night even though their bellies were full. My mother and her siblings would be like flies on the wall while trying to listen to grown folk conversation and gossip. My grandmother had a couple of friends that were overweight who would talk about the latest trends in weight loss.

"Louise, girl you look so nice, where did you say you got those diet pills you've been taking?" Betty asked.

"I got them at the drugstore and as you can see, they work! I've lost fifteen pounds so far." Louise replied.

When my mother learned about how easy it was to get her hands on some diet pills, she went to the drug store right away and started taking them to make a good impression on Larry. She knew she had to do something to be able to compete with the other girls for his attention. After losing twenty pounds, she had an "aw ha" moment and realized that she could have what she wanted in life if she put her mind to it. She strategized to get Larry's attention by making sure she was where he hung out. She knew all the places and her quest to be in his presence was easy since they had a lot of mutual friends. He lived in her neighborhood, and his house was a few short blocks away from my grandparents. My mother got a glimpse of him every day.

Larry had a huge ego, he knew that he was attractive and most of the girls wanted his attention. My mother listened to all the rumors that circulated the neighborhood about his sexual conquest, but it didn't stop her. It was no secret that he was a player. When Larry noticed that my mother was trying to get his attention, he made her work hard before letting on that he was interested. She wore tight fitting clothing like the other girls and make-up. The other boys began flirting with her and commenting on how good she looked. Her confidence and self-esteem got a boost. However, Larry's made her feel uncomfortable. She found it hard to believe that he was willing to forgo some of the most attractive girls around the way, to be with her.

After passing by his house for what seemed like two weeks straight, Larry finally yelled out to my mother and she tried to act coy.

"Girl if you keep strolling your fine ass pass here I'm going to drag you inside and get me some."

"What are you talking about? I'm looking for my brothers, they play basketball over there, besides you don't own the neighborhood."

"True, but you ain't fooling nobody, you're out here looking for me. Anyone can see that."

My mother laughed nervously knowing that what he said was true. He continued to flirt with her before inviting her to his house. She agreed to go inside. Larry assumed that she wanted to mess around. He didn't want to engage in small talk there was one thing he wanted from her like most mannish young men his age.

"Julie, you're looking good today, and those pants are hugging your ass just the way they were made to. Girl, I know you want me I've been watching you." He told her. "I don't know about that, I told you I been coming around here to watch my brothers play basketball." My mother replied.

"Don't be nervous, I'd like to get to know you better," he said as he grabbed her hand and rubbed it over his manhood.

My mother tried to relax, as she stood in the middle of his living room taking in the beautiful décor. His family had a reputation for having nice things, and he always wore cute clothes. As she stood there following his lead, she knew there was no turning back. She felt confident in her tight-fitting jeans, and they did hug her butt perfectly as Larry alluded to. She purposely wore underwear that matched her bra. He kissed her while unbuttoning her jeans and she knew if she didn't go all the way he'd move on to the next girl.

Her heart was beating fast. It felt like it was going to bust out of her chest, so she tried to distract him by asking "Where are your parents?"

"They went to church. They won't be back for a while." He told her.

The young man who my mother chased was now chasing her, and he expected her to put out. Larry led her out to his garage believing that it would be the best place to hear his parents if they came back home early.

"If you hear a car pull up, you'll need to grab your clothes and get out of here fast. Believe me, you don't want my mother to catch you in here." His mother was a religious woman who didn't like little hot girls coming around flirting with her son. He pointed to the side door in the corner so she'd know how to exit if necessary. Larry continued taking her clothes off while placing tender kisses on her lips. Her knees began to buckle. Although she was inexperienced and nervous, she allowed Larry to have his way with her. He gently pushed her up against the freezer while easing himself inside her. She held on tight as he went deeper causing her to moan. She couldn't believe how he made her feel in the moment and wished the feeling could last forever.

Unfortunately, their first sexual encounter would be their last. Larry got what he wanted from her and added her name to his list of conquests. His desire to continue her game of cat and mouse was over. Although she hoped that he would remain interested, she knew he was going to move on to the next girl. Days later she felt disappointed after seeing him looking out his window as she passed his house only to be ignored by him. She cried whenever she saw him with another girl on his arms or heard more rumors about him. She hoped that her name wouldn't be part of them. His behavior was difficult to swallow causing her to sink back into her mundane life of living in the shadows of others.

It didn't take long for my mother to gain the weight back that she had lost. Her hips began to spread, and her breast was getting larger by the day. She assumed the weight gain was from not taking her diet pills. In fact, she had stopped taking them after Larry stopped paying attention to her. She missed two periods and put two and two together realizing she was pregnant. "Now what?" She thought to herself, knowing that Larry wasn't the type who was ready to be a father to anybody's child. She didn't want to tell him and decided to keep her pregnancy a secret from everyone.

At this juncture, my mother was depressed and felt alone. Larry had warned her during their brief encounter about getting pregnant.

"Don't think that getting pregnant will keep me," he said.

"I'm not, a baby is the last thing I want," she told him, to change the subject.

My mother knew he meant what he said and wouldn't stick around. Lots of girls were getting pregnant by young men who had no intentions of being in a relationship or marrying them. Larry wanted to chase girls and not get tied down by them.

My mother was consumed with worry about herself and her unborn child. She laid in her bed for days wondering how she was going to tell my grandmother about her situation. She couldn't trust her sisters with her secret and decided to hide her pregnancy well into her eighth month. My grandmother had no idea she was going to be helping raise another child. She found out soon enough after my mother fell down a flight of stairs inside their house forcing her to tell. My mother believed that her baby's life was in danger.

She frantically yelled for my grandmother while attempting to pick herself up. She broke the news with hopes to gain confidence and establish help with her situation. My grandmother in the kitchen preparing dinner while humming familiar tunes like she often did.

"Mama I'm pregnant," she blurted out while searching my grandmother's face to gauge her reaction.

"Child how long you been hiding this?" My grandmother asked.

"I haven't had my period in months. I was scared to tell you. I think I'm pretty far along," she said as tears rolled down her face.

"This is serious! Grab your sweater and come on, we've got to get you in to see a doctor." My grandmother demanded.

"Yes mama," my mother said as she followed her instructions.

My grandmother acted being fully aware that it wasn't the time to be judgmental or to ask questions like "who was the baby's father?" Instead, she and my mother headed downtown to the clinic. My mother desperately needed prenatal care but they were turned away when they got there. The clerk told them that there was only one doctor on duty and it was almost closing time. The doctor wasn't seeing any more patients. This caused my grandmother some concern. In her mind, it was an emergency, and she was agitated. She considered lashing out at the clerk but concluded the woman was just doing her job.

"Don't worry Julie, somebody's gonna help us today even if we have to go to the emergency room." My grandmother assured her.

They decided to try another clinic that was located around the corner from the first one. My grandmother clutched my mother's hand tightly as they walked there. She assured her that everything was going to be alright. They went to St. Ann's Clinic, a well-known clinic in the community that served low-income families and never turned anyone away. When they walked in, they were greeted by an older woman manning the front desk. They quickly walked towards her to get help.

"Excuse me, can you please help us? My pregnant daughter fell down a flight of stairs earlier today. I think she's pretty far along." My grandmother reported.

"Yes, of course, we can help! Fill out these forms, and I'll get her back to see the doctor as soon as possible," the clerk said while pointing to the waiting area. They patiently waited for my mother's name to be called.

"Julie Fitzgerald" a slender woman called out. She led them back to the examining room.

"Julie, I need to take your vitals and to ask a few questions." The nurse reported. "What caused you to fall and when exactly did it happen."

"I fell today while attempting to vacuum. I was standing too close to the steps and lost my footing." My mother explained.

"Are you in any pain?"

"Yes, my hip hurts, and I have rug burns on my arms."

"Go ahead and get completely undressed. Put this grown on and leave the back open because we need to run a few tests."

My mother followed the nurse's instructions as my grandmother helped her to get up on the examining table. They waited in silence for the doctor to come into the room. My mother shivered from being cold and nervous, not knowing what to expect. It was only a matter of minutes before the doctor knocked on the door to enter the room.

"Good Afternoon, I'm Dr. Blackwell, what brings you in today?"

"I'm pregnant, but I'm sure you already know that. I was hiding it from my parents but panicked after I fell today. My feet came from underneath me causing me to fall down the stairs. I am afraid I may have harmed my baby."

"Well, you've done the right thing by coming in. Can you please lay back on the table so that I can examine you?"

My mother followed the doctor's instructions and hoped her baby was okay. After Dr. Blackwell completed the exam, he told my mother that she and her baby were fine.

"It looks like you're about thirty-six weeks pregnant or thereabouts. I've listened to the baby's heartbeat, and I didn't hear anything abnormal, but I would like for you to take a few extra tests just to be on the safe side. My nurse will come back in a few minutes to start them."

My grandmother was perplexed; the look on her face told the whole story. She tried to process what the doctor said about how far along my mother was in her pregnancy. She thought it was one thing for her to have missed a few periods, but another to be having a baby in a matter of weeks. Her family would be welcoming a new Fitzgerald into their home. The situation caused her a lot of anxiety, but she tried to remain calm.

"Lord help us," she muttered as she unconsciously rolled her eyes at my mother.

My mother realized that her pregnancy was going to be a life-changing event for everyone concerned. The nurse returned to run the tests that were ordered. My mother studied her face for clues before she shared her findings. She told my mother that the baby's vital signs were good and the baby was positioned with its head down. The world stopped as my mother took a few minutes to process what she was saying. The nurse confirmed that my mother's baby wasn't in danger and that she would be delivering a healthy child in a matter of weeks. The nurse also provided her with a referral to see an Obstetrician in the area who could monitor her pregnancy until it was time to give birth.

My mother learned a fundamental lesson that day. No matter how difficult things are, you should always tell the truth. There was one more person who needed to know what was going on and it was my grand-dad. My grandmother was worried about how he would react, and my mother was concerned about how he would feel about her becoming a teen mom. My grandmother suggested they wait before telling him, she figured he wouldn't notice her growing belly since he was always working. My grandmother told my mother the best way to avoid him was to stay in her room unless it was dinnertime. Her plan seemed to work.

My grandmother blamed herself for my mother's dilemma and tried to do everything she could to help her. She felt terrible whenever she'd heard my mother crying profusely in her bedroom. She began to feel ill from all the stress and took action by coming up with a grandiose scheme. She and my grand-dad loved hosting red-light cabaret parties in their basement. Family and friends would congregate down there to listen to the record player. They'd enjoy Smokey Robinson and the Miracles, The Supremes, and other soulful singers. A lot of slow dragging and drinking went on down there. If you let my grandmother tell it, the basement was her favorite place to escape to. It was where she'd go to take a few swigs of alcohol whenever she got the notion, then sneak back upstairs to take care of her family. Everyone suspected her of being a "drunk" because of the way she slurred her words, but no one was brave enough to confront her. One day, while she snuck away to get a quick sip of Vodka, she decided to read the label. The potency of her favorite drink was so strong you'd pass out after one drink if you were an amateur. She had developed a tolerance for strong alcohol over the years. That peaked her interest, so she read the labels of the other types of alcohol that were behind the bar that included Whiskies, Rums, and Vodkas. The 80 proof Vodka was going to have to do the trick. She believed that if my mother drank it, the potency would be stronger enough to cause her to abort her baby. She felt everyone would be better off if my mother didn't have a baby.

"Julie come down here and help me with these clothes," my grandmother yelled.

Judging by her tone, my mother hurried down the steps to see what the matter was. The familiar sound meant if you didn't respond quickly there would be hell to pay.

"Coming," my mother said as she waddled down the stairs to see what she wanted.

"Hurry up drink this," my grandmother demanded.

"What is it? My mother asked knowing all along that it was the white alcohol she seen the adults enjoying in the basement.

"Shhhhhhh, just drink it," she demanded.

My mother took the half-full bottle of Vodka, turned it up mimicking the adults, took a few gulps, and spewed it out on the floor. The strong taste sickened her.

"I can't-do this mama" she pleaded.

"Drink it, child, I'm trying to help you! Here try again." She said as she grabbed the bottle and attempted to pour some in my mother's mouth.

My mother continued to gag. She found it impossible to keep it down long enough for the scheme to work. My grandmother became furious with her because she couldn't control the situation. The reality was another grandchild was on the way, and she was going to have to deal with it. My mother was in disbelief! She couldn't believe her mother would try to abort her baby. She felt sick to her stomach but was grateful that she couldn't keep the alcohol down. It was apparent that God had a plan for my destiny and my grandmother didn't have the power to change it. The experience caused my mother to have a renewed appreciation for the life she was bringing into the world. She vowed to follow her doctor's instructions to the letter until it was time for me to make my debut.

My grandmother wasn't willing to go through the harsh judgment families received whenever their teen or unmarried daughter's get pregnant in their communities. She and my grand-dad had already seen firsthand how their daughter Gayle, my mother's sister was ostracized after becoming pregnant with my cousin Kimberly. Folks were downright nasty. My grandmother had no other choice but to tell grand-dad, she didn't want to blindside him by bringing another screaming newborn into their home.

"Owen, Julie is pregnant," she blurted out one evening as they sat on the porch enjoying the breeze.

"No, not my Julie!" My grand-dad protested.

"I'm sorry honey, but it's true, Julie is having a baby soon."

"Dammit woman, I asked you to keep a better eye on our girls. How could you allow this to happen again? You're home with them every day?"

"Honey, it's not the time to point fingers. I can't be with Julie twenty-four hours a day."

"I know, but I would have never thought this would happen to Julie. I'm sorry for lashing out at you, but we're barely making ends meet, and now you're telling me there will be another mouth to feed?" My grand-dad realized that making a fuss wasn't going to help solve anything, and it wasn't my grandmother's fault that my mother got pregnant.

The remainder of my mom's pregnancy was smooth. Our family warmed up to the idea of having a new baby around. On August 11, 1970, my mother began having contractions. She told my grandparents, and they rushed her to the hospital where she was admitted. Her contractions were getting closer, and the nurse said it wasn't going to be long before my mother would be told to push. She cooperated with the staff the best she could even though the pain was getting the best of her. When she finally dilated ten centimeters she gave one push.

"You can do it! Give me one more big push," the doctor said.

Grappled with a lot of pain and the desire to make it go away my mother gave her final push.

"It's a girl!" the doctor announced as they quickly took me away to clean me up.

At 8:15 PM, I Kalena Marcell Fitzgerald, made my debut into the world. I weighed 5lbs and had a head full of jet black hair. Everyone made a fuss over me and said I was beautiful. My mother had mixed emotions, but my grandparents fell in love with me at first sight. Their shame dissipated as they welcomed me into their home once my mom was discharged from the hospital. I believe she was courageous for having me at such a young age. I'm sure it wasn't easy for her with all her insecurities staring her in the face along with worrying about if she would be a good mom.

Although my mother received a lot of help from my grandparents and her sisters, it was difficult for her to form a bond with me, but I'll give her credit for trying. My early memories of her are vague; however, I recall hearing her angelic voice as it filled the room. The melodies she sang always gave me comfort especially when she sang Judy Garland's "Somewhere Over the Rainbow." The lyrics resonated with me. My mother's voice created a reality and expectation of the world I lived in along with all of its magical possibilities. I realized early on that to survive, I would have to embrace my power and walk confidently in it. As a young girl, I realized that words have meaning and there's a real art to communication. Words matter, so you should be careful of what you say especially when raising children. Your actions can become a self-fulfilling prophecy.

As a child, I realized that Julie was my mother, even though my grandmother took over the role as mom since my mother was still learning the ropes. I considered my grandparents my parents, and it was easy for me to call them mom and dad since everyone else did. I felt disconnected from my mother; she remained distant while we lived with my grandparents. When my brother Dwight was born, a year after me, my grandparents embraced him too. I'm not sure if they went through the same heartache they experienced when my mother got pregnant with me, but I suspect by the third grandchild they were used to it.

I loved living in my grandparent's crowded house. I felt a sense of independence and power there. It was electrifying! Every day seemed better than the last. Raising children with strong family values was second nature for my grandparents. They were pillars of our community, and everyone respected them. There were ten Fitzgerald's in our house: my grandparents, their five children, my brother, cousin, and me. We didn't have a lot, but the love we shared couldn't be replaced.

I don't recall there being a lot of talk in our house about Dwight's father or mine; however, we knew they weren't around. I learned later in life that my mother kept in contact with my daddy, Larry Hullum until around my second birthday. She still carried a torch for him even though they had a contentious relationship; however, he burnt his bridges with her after asking to borrow fifty dollars. Although she didn't believe his story about why he needed the money, and he had turned his back on her years before, she was still willing to hand over fifty bucks believing it was the thing that could reignite their flame but Larry hadn't changed he still was up to no good. He got her money, ran off to California and married a mutual friend. His actions reinforced the fact that he was "no good" and she needed to unleash the hold he had over her.

She needed to get over him and focus on raising her children without a man.

My mother lived with my grandparents for a few more years. After my grand-dad lost his job as a truck driver, it forced our family to move to a less desirable neighborhood on the other side of town. They moved to 104 Elliot Street off 93rd and Union, which didn't sit too well with their children who believed they were too good to live in the ghetto. Suddenly the Fitzgerald household got smaller! My aunts and uncles moved out, my Uncle Danny went off to college, and Aunt Gayle and Precious went to live with my grandmother's sister, Aunt Gwenie. My grand-dad secured a job at Sears, Roebuck & Company, and continued to work hard to provide for his family. It didn't take us long to get acclimated to our new neighborhood, which was diverse. Many of the people who live there didn't look like me, but I found it refreshing and acknowledged the differences. I was naturally curious and wanted to learn all I could about different cultures. There were no color barriers, Germans, Polish, Caucasians, and Hispanics all lived in harmony.

I recall a sweet little black lady who lived next door to us in a white two-story house made of wooden shingles with a large front porch. I had to climb up five steps just to see her. She was a brown-skinned woman in her late sixties or early seventies who weighted around one hundred pounds. She was frail and more than likely suffered from arthritis or osteoporosis. When she walked hunched over, all I could do was fixate on her beauty. She went to the beauty parlor every week to get her hair done. She wore her thin length hair in beautiful pin curls and reminded me of my grandmother.

We developed a special connection. I'd voluntarily go to her house and knock on the door to see if she wanted my company. When she did, she'd invite me to sit on the porch with here where we'd eat apples. She had them ready for us, and they were delicious! I'd run over there every chance I got because I felt safe there. I loved how she respected my power and paid attention to me even though I was a child. She taught me that I was free to share my opinions, and she'd encourage me to let some steam off my chest which was mostly some rant about my brother's bad behavior or my grandmother's stern nature.

"You'll be better off someday for listening to your grandparents, baby," she said.

Having her trust really helped me to step firmly into the shoes God gave me to fill. She allowed me to daydream about a brighter future. Sometimes we'd sit in silence, and others she would do the talking. I loved to listen to her talk about her late husband and her children who lived in other parts in the city.

"I really miss my Darnell," she said as her eyes filled up with tears. She'd quickly change the subject to hear more about what I wanted to talk about.

"Tell me about your day Kalena?" she'd say.

I was always hoping that she was really interested in knowing the details because once I started; my rants resembled "tell all" newspapers from a child's perspective. Being in her company reminded me that the world according to Kalena was exactly the way it was supposed to be. I had a voice and a choice in the outcome of my life. After telling her my worldview, I'd run back home and assimilate into the life that seemed normal to me.

The thing I remember most about my grandparents' house was everyone pitched in to help without expecting something in return. Dwight and I always had what we needed; my aunts and uncles made themselves available to help my grandparents take care of us. They never made a fuss about whose responsibility it was. Our house resembled a hodgepodge of grown-ups, pets, and children. Delicious meals were being cooked daily. The aroma of homemade recipes being prepared by my grandmother lingered in the air whenever she cooked. We craved her specialties like French Toast, Banana Pudding, homemade Pickles, and Cucumbers and Onions marinate in vinegar. I loved to watch her cooking and wanted to be taught. My goal was to get invited to receive some cooking lessons. I wanted bragging rights and to rub them in the faces of Dwight and Kimberly. To this day, I still cherish her recipes and have passed down a few to my daughter.

I received my first glimpse of what a traditional family looked like while living with my grandparents. I depended on them for guidance. Being four years old, in a house with adults, didn't lend itself to being disrespectful or noisy when it came to adult business without some type of consequence. We were taught by our grandparents to stay in a child's place. I could enjoy the things that were at my eye level like the dogs, cats, and the fishes in the aquarium. Our pets were playmates. The fish belonged to my grandmother, and she loved them. She would make a fuss if we forgot to feed them. Her love for fish is something that she passed on to me. I too am a fish lover! As a child, I told myself that I would have fish in my home once I became an adult.

One of my favorite pastimes as a five-year-old was watching television in our living room. We had one of those old fashion floor model TV's, you know the one, "the boob tube" that looked like a buffet table. It didn't matter if I was the only one watching it; I had to see my favorite television show "Alice". Boy, could she keep my attention with her sassy attitude. I loved to mimic and repeat her outlandish catchphrase "kiss my grits." She said it to Al a lot especially when he made her mad. I was good at it and saying those three words made me feel powerful.

Dwight would pretend he was my audience and laugh until his stomach hurt as I carried on.

I dared myself to repeat her infamous words to an adult and believed that it would be fun to try it on my grand-dad because he had a good sense of humor. I assumed that he would appreciate my impression of Alice. I was wrong! My smart mouth earned me my first and last whooping by him. My grand-dad never and I mean never raised a hand to whoop any of his children or grandchildren. That day he caught me by surprise when he whooped me for being mouthy and not knowing the gravity of my assertion. Remember the rule, children need to stay in their place.

"Kiss my Grits Grand-pa," I said to him with pride before running out the front door to play. I felt proud of myself since I had just unloaded some of my sassiness that Alice taught me. He didn't even blink, and he allowed me to think everything was okay. However, he felt that I had insulted him and he waited patiently for me to come back inside. I ran through the front door with a sweatband on my forehead thirsty and tired from playing with the boys in the neighborhood. My grand-dad was sitting in the hallway next to the front door. The expression he had on his face wasn't familiar to me, but I could tell that he was brewing over something. It didn't take long for him to let me know exactly what was on his mind.

"Come here for a minute Kalena, I have to tell you something," he said.

"What grandpa," I uttered still being sassy.

Before I knew it, he grabbed me by the arm while attempting to pull my pants down and delivered to me a whooping. I tried to wiggle loose but his grip was firm. You could hear a pin drop as everyone inside the house gasped and listened to me getting my tail beat. I had no idea why I was being spanked and why no one told him to stop. Of course, I cried louder than necessary, but he had an attitude and wasn't going to allow me to get free until he was finished making his point. I learned my lesson that day.

My grandmother told me that saying, "kiss my grits" was disrespectful and I needed to apologize. She said she was going to wash my mouth out with soap and reminded me that my grand-dad wasn't the only one capable of disciplining me.

"Dry up those tears and go apologize to your grand-dad," my grandmother demanded.

"Yes ma'am," I replied as I tried to gather my composure.

My grand-dad gave me a hug and told me that he wasn't angry with me anymore. I think he felt bad that he had to whoop his favorite grandchild. Needless to say, I was embarrassed and vowed never to be spanked by him again. I had a problem with pride as a child, and my pride wouldn't allow me to be seen crying in front of my family a second time. They knew I had a tough exterior and it was hard to get me to cry. I never wanted anyone to feel like they had something on me, not even my family.

My infatuation with life while living at my grandparents' house didn't last long, things suddenly came to a screeching halt when my mother announced that she was ready to live life on her own terms and without the support of my grandparents. She wanted to build a life with her boyfriend, Frank, and believed that he was the perfect man for her since he was willing to accept Dwight and me as his own children. I knew there would be some bumps in the road, but exactly how many, I didn't know.

CHAPTER 1

Reflection

There are a lot of feelings that come to mind when I look back on my childhood. Things at my eye level seemed to be airy, playful, free, bright, and full in my young mind. My grandparents' house was full of people and animals. I felt safe and secure living there. As a child, we are invited into this world, and we don't have a choice of who our parents will be or even the ability to determine their lifestyles: wealthy or poor or better or worse. We can't choose the dynamics and don't know if our home will reflect stability, instability, violence, or all these things simultaneously. Things were perfect at my grandparents' house- it was my "normal." Their house was both functional and dysfunctional! There was a workaholic grand-dad, an alcoholic grandmother, a distant mother who was an unwed mother, and no father in the home. As a child, these things aren't important until someone tells you they are or when parents don't have the answers to the pressing needs of their child as they grow and develop. I learned to be mouthy, it was the only way I felt that I would be heard and it ultimately became a protective mechanism for me. Being mouthy got me in a lot of trouble with my elders because during that era growing up in some African American household children were taught to stay in their place which meant you were seen and not heard.

The little lady who lived next door along with my grandparents helped me to establish my identity by listening to their wisdom. I was drawn to their conversations and respected their worldview. It helped to shape me. My family introduced me to a diverse world and to embrace different cultures, German, Indian, and African American alike. I recall experiencing a spiritual awakening around the age of five. It started when I became drawn to the Bible. I tried to read it even though I was too young to comprehend it on a spiritual level but realized that I would need the teachings to navigate through life. I was consciously learning and expecting to receive ideas about myself or who I was through my examples I saw in the adults who I loved.

CHAPTER 2

Power Discovered

My life changed drastically when my mother's boyfriend, Frank, convinced her that they should live together. She was infatuated with him and believed that he was the key to helping her gain her independence from my grandparents. Frank was an honest, hardworking man who was from our neighborhood, he lived a few blocks down the street. Their relationship wasn't frowned upon even though racism still existed back in the 70's. Frank was a handsome white man who kept a neatly groomed mustache and beard. He was average height and weight, which didn't match up to his mean demeanor. He thought he was tough because he grew up in a predominantly black area. He hung out with my uncles, and they thought he was cool.

Frank convinced my mother that he could provide her with the lifestyle she desired; once they started dating, they had a whirlwind romance. In the beginning, he was good for her self-esteem and always told her that she was pretty. He spent a lot of time with her which was something that she wasn't used to. He convinced her he'd be a loving father figure for us. My mother wanted Dwight and me to have a father, and Frank was saying all the things she wanted to hear.

It wasn't my place to judge Frank, I was a child, but I wished someone had asked my opinion because my power would've kicked in and I'd tell them that I wasn't impressed by him. In fact, he reminded me of a "red neck" because he always wore wife beaters and flannel shirts. He was a chain smoker who kept a cigarette in one hand and a 32oz mug of coffee in the other. My mother allowed Frank to discipline us without question and he did every chance he got. He was quick to anger, and for some reason, I was always his target. He realized early on that I had a pretty tough exterior, and reprimanding me was going to be challenging. I couldn't put my finger on what made Frank tick, but I believed that he simply didn't like Dwight and me although he had just made a commitment to our mother to provide a better life for us. He took an issue with most of the things we did and even things that we didn't, he blamed on us. I started to resent him and told myself that I'd eventually get even.

Frank had a bad habit of asking me every Saturday morning to get him a cup of coffee. Since he drank it often, he'd ask several times throughout the day which continued into Sundays morning. He had no idea that I was plotting against him and wanted to resign as his personal coffee girl.

"Kalena, fill my mug back up." He'd say.

I'd sigh, and follow his instructions. I'd take his stained 32oz. sunflower yellow Tupperware cup with the dark coffee ring, and go into the kitchen and reach for the coffee pot to refill his cup. Most of the time, I wouldn't tamper with its contents, but there were a few times I gave his coffee a secret ingredient. I'd sprinkle just a little comet in his cup and stir his coffee. It was occasional and without malice of course. My intent wasn't to make him sick or murder him; I just wanted to get even. I felt my power and wanted the upper hand. I was tired of being his little coffee girl and figured that if I altered the taste, he'd stopping asking, but he didn't. Surprisingly he never detected the taste of the comet, and I never told a soul.

I began to notice that when my mother was around Frank, she behaved differently. She was at his beck and call; consequentially that meant Dwight and I received less of her attention. She'd start her day around 6am and would head to the kitchen to cook Frank breakfast before he went to work. Bacon, eggs, and toast were always on the menu, and the smell of his hot breakfast woke me up like an automatic alarm clock. The smell still reminds me of home. The sad part about those mornings was we weren't offered a hot breakfast of bacon and eggs which forced me to assume that my mother didn't think we were good enough for them. Frank eating this type of food didn't sit too well with me because he didn't seem to mind that he was the only one who was able to enjoy it. One day I overheard him tell my mother that he thought he was too good to eat cereal. The thought of him being a white man who was sitting on his high perch looking down on the people he was supposed to love made me furious.

I'd sit there day after day, daydreaming about what bacon and eggs tasted like and didn't find out until I was a teenager. Dwight and I were served a cold breakfast that consisted of corn flakes with milk. My mother's desire to be comfortable in a home she and Frank built together was more important than her children. Her desire was to make him happy and to minimize the conflicts between them that started at the drop of a hat demonstrated to me that she was powerless. I knew my mother wasn't living or operating in her power by catering to Frank.

I didn't realize how poor we were even though Frank worked a full-time job. My mother could stretch a dollar to feed and clothe us. There were times when she'd take grocery items like milk and pour half its contents into two empty jugs then fill the rest with either water or powdered milk. We'd use the watered-down milk to eat our Corn Flakes. The taste was awful yet tolerable. We had no other options, but to eat what was provided or go hungry. I hated it, it was mentally frustrating and not to mention seeing other options in the fridge, but not at liberty to touch them made me want to take up the issue with her, but I was smarter than that and knew my place.

I had a lot of pride, and no matter the circumstance I told myself a different story even though I couldn't back up my assumption of not being poor. I learned the power of positive self-talk, and it worked for me. I never told the kids at school about my home life, or about how frugal my mother was because it would be a negative reflection of me. I thank God that she dressed us in new or gently worn clothes. My friends thought I was spoiled and had the 'good' life.

It wasn't long before Frank asked my mother to marry him but the idea didn't sit too well with me. I was glad that my grandparents lived a few houses down from us making it easy to go there to escape my reality. I suppressed my feelings and didn't let anyone know I thought Frank was a fake. It would have been pointless anyway since I was a child. I believed their union would cause me more stress and feelings of alienation. I couldn't find my place in the home I was told was mine. I was the oldest and the only girl who was being treated poorly by my mother. I couldn't win! Whenever I felt discouraged, I'd rely on my positive self-talk to pick me up, and I'd get a resurgence of power.

My mother couldn't wait for her wedding day. I recall it like it was yesterday; it took place in my grandparents' living room. My mother had been excited for weeks and had taken us shopping to make sure Dwight and I looked perfect on her special day. She allowed me to pick out a frilly white dress and brought me black patent leather shoes to match. I couldn't wait to put on that dress, and once I did, I felt pretty. My mother took time to curl my hair perfectly so I could look beautiful like her. It was one of the few times I remember her connecting with me, and her timing could not have been better. I was thrilled to have her attention.

My grandmother and aunts made a fuss over my mother as she got dressed. They made sure she looked perfect on her special day. We dressed ourselves at my grandparents' house, and Frank stayed home to get ready. When he arrived, he looked polished in his new sky-blue suit. His black hair was slicked back, and his shoes were shinier than a brand-new penny. He ditched his wife beaters and flannel shirts to marry my mother that day. He strolled into my grandparent's living room with a sense of renewed confidence. He was ready to take his vows in front of our family and God. When he saw me, he rushed over and picked me up as if he hadn't seen me in weeks. He gave me a big hug. I was perplexed by his behavior because he hadn't acted that way before. Looking back, I believe it was his way of letting me know that I was special to him. I felt happy to be with my family, but I still wasn't happy about the wedding.

I couldn't wait for their ceremony to end. I was ready for the reception in the basement. Our family embraced Frank and welcomed him with opened arms. My mother was glowing she seemed so happy. I thought she looked beautiful, but I kept it to myself. I walked through the house prancing around in my frilly white dress hoping everyone saw me. I was looking for compliments. My grandparents were the first to feed my ego and told me that I looked pretty. I disappeared into the small crowd for what seemed like forever until Dwight tapped me on my shoulder to say our mother was looking for me.

"Kalena mama wants you," he said. "She's in the kitchen and said hurry up!"

"What does she want," I asked. Dwight ran off without providing an answer.

My mother was standing in the kitchen just like Dwight said she would be and didn't waste time leading me into an empty corner by the refrigerator for privacy. She got right to the point.

"Kalena, now that I'm married to Frank, you can start calling him dad now," she said. "He really does love you and your brother."

"Yes mama," I said while looking up at the ceiling.

I pretended to agree with her, but what she was asking of me wasn't going to fly. I gave her a fake smile to avoid ruining her day even though I was confused. I was only six years old, but I was old enough to know that Frank wasn't my real dad besides we hadn't known him that long. Suddenly, it was important to our mother that we pretend like Frank was our dad. I called him dad right away just to please her, but it made me feel incomplete, I was still a fatherless daughter who was giving up some of my power to follow my mother's request. I did my best to enjoy the rest of her wedding day, and when it was time for everyone to go down to the basement, I shoved my way to the front of the crowd to claim my favorite spot in the corner by the bar where all the alcohol was housed. I climbed up on the backless barstool made of metal. It had a round red vinyl seat that I love to twirl around on to see everything. It was the best seat in the house for me to observe the grownups dance, and carry on. I recall how beautiful they decorated the basement. My Uncle Fred, who was my granddads brother who looked just like him but taller and skinnier, noticed me in the corner and came over to ask why I wasn't playing with the rest of the kids.

"Kalena, what are you doing over here in the corner, you should be having fun with your cousins, but I guess if you want to sit over here it's okay by me. What would you like to drink?" He asked.

"I'll have a coke and orange juice," I said trying to mimic something that I heard the grown-ups order on many occasions. My uncle gave me that look that grown-ups give because he thought I was being sassy. He laughed as he walked away to get me what I ordered.

"Here you go, drink up but don't let me see you sitting here all night you hear me." He warned.

"Don't worry Uncle Fred you'll see Dwight and me dancing later," I said.

I didn't hesitate to start sipping my drink with my pinky finger extended. I loved observing my grandparents, aunts and uncles, and particularly my mother and Frank whenever there was a party in the basement. The parties were lively, and the love everyone shared will never escape my memory. My mother's reception seemed to last forever, everyone was having a good time drinking, dancing, and taking pictures. My grandmother told Dwight and me that we needed to get ready for bed since we were spending the night. She wanted to give my mother and Frank some alone time since they weren't going on a honeymoon. I noticed how good my mother and Frank were getting along. They couldn't keep their hands off each other, but I was smart enough to know that it was the calm before the storm. Once we returned to our everyday life, there would be more rocky days to maneuver.

With all the wedding hoopla over with, we settled in as a family. My mother had a new set of expectations for Frank as her husband and sought a kinder version of his previous self. However, she would soon be disappointed because the honeymoon didn't last long. The first thing I noticed was the warm, secure feeling I'd come to appreciate at my grandparents' house, didn't exist at ours. Although, Frank's face beamed with joy wherever he heard Dwight and I call him dad, I couldn't seem to shake the uneasiness I felt in his presence. I placed most of the blame for the situation squarely on my mother's shoulders because she failed to protect me. She never asked me if I did something or spoke kindly to me, she always demanded. It bothered me that she was always forcing my brother and me to adjust, conform, and except things. I never got to have an opinion. Getting married didn't change her behavior it remained the same. We didn't get any quality time with her, and she still struggled to show affection. I craved a relationship with her and prayed that she would be different especially since I was her only daughter. I bet the reason she acted the way she did was she too had a desire to receive more attention from my grandparents as a child.

It wasn't long before my mother and Frank's relationship hit the rocks. I felt a lot of tension forming between them. The accusations, verbal abuse, and domestic violence were traumatizing. I was old enough to be affected by the mayhem. I knew my mother was in pain, but there wasn't anything I could do about it. I wondered why things had to be that way and questioned why she couldn't tap into her power.

Most of their disagreements stemmed from Frank's dissatisfaction with our behavior. After warm and fuzzy feelings wore off, my mother started to defend us, but that made the situation more threatening. Their fights were always in earshot, and it wasn't unusual for Dwight and me to hear plates being flung up against the wall then shattering into a thousand pieces. Frank had a bad temper that could escalate at the drop of a hat. He'd walk around slamming doors, physically abusing with my mother, and verbally insulting her. I experienced a lot of trauma, but I didn't want to tell my grandparents what was going on. I suspect they already knew but wanted to mind their own business. Frank acted like he was bipolar. He had an ugly side and a sweet one. I loved to see him when he was in a good mood which was rare. He and my mother would act like teenagers in love. It wasn't long before she became pregnant with my brother John, but his birth didn't seem to help their marriage, in fact, their arguments intensified. Frank was a bully. I learned to blanket myself from what I saw and heard. It was another way I was able to build up a tough exterior. I couldn't protect my brothers I felt paralyzed in the moment, and helpless whenever I heard them crying at night after hearing one of Frank and my mothers' nasty fights. I wanted to protect them, but I was just a child with limited power.

My self-esteem began taking some hits. My mother was sending a message to me, her only daughter that it was okay to be a victim of domestic violence and stay with the perpetrator. I started wetting the bed because of the emotional distress I was under. I didn't want anyone to know so I'd get up in the middle of the night and change my sheets and clothes. I wasn't going to allow my mother or Frank to find out about it. They had enough ammunition to use against me, and I wasn't going to let them win. They never figured out about my bedwetting episodes that lasted until I was around eight years old.

When they weren't fighting, Frank and my mother was making babies. My mother found out that she was pregnant again with my brother Tavis. She had four small children to look after and to compete for her time and attention of our mother. Frank insisted that she stayed at home like my grandmother did to raise us. As time went on, she began to feel trapped and continued to put up with Frank's antics. I believe that she didn't think she could do any better. He was a man's man who demanded respect from everybody. As my brothers got older, they did everything to please him. They needed his validation, but I didn't, I yearned to have the acceptance and love of my own daddy who was out there somewhere in the big world. I didn't understand why he abandoned me, but I wanted to know his side of the story.

I did my best to avoid my mother and Franks' wrath. However, when they needed someone to pick on, I always felt that I was at the brunt of it, they always tried to attack my self-worth. I think in some ways I reminded my mother of my daddy, and I use to think she wanted to pin all his wrongdoings on me; it wasn't fair. The names she called me were probably a reflection of the way she viewed herself. Dwight and I formed an alliance. We were close and tried our best to protect one another. He was the one person I could trust and could confide in. Our bond grew stronger once we started school.

We went to school at Mt. Pleasant Elementary School. Back then it wasn't surprising to see small children walking to school. My mother taught us how to get there safely, and we memorized the best route. She and Frank only had one vehicle, and he needed it to get back and forth to work. My mother timed us; she had confidence in us, but warned us about stranger danger. She told us not to talk to them and to always be aware of our surroundings.

We'd walk from 104th Street and Union to 116th Street and Union which was one of the busiest intersections in Cleveland. I wasn't afraid, as a child, I didn't understand the risks of being a little girl living in a dangerous world. There were consequences if you didn't pay attention. I was caught up in my own existence, which consisted of searching for a brighter world with vibrant colors and assuming that everyone who lived in it is a good person. Being able to make it home safely made me feel powerful at an early age. Those early years helped to shape my ability to become more mature than most kids my age.

Dwight and I were also rebellious, we did a lot of stuff and got away with it. We believed that getting some attention from our mother even if it was negative was better than nothing. She had become less tolerable of our bad behavior. She needed to keep things simple since raising four children close in age wasn't easy. We were expected to be independent, and she demanded that we help around the house. More importantly, we were responsible for getting ourselves dressed for school and making it there on time. I recall the day Dwight and I decided to test the limits by not coming straight home from school. We loved to play outside and at school on the gym equipment. We decided to do just that, by staying after school to play instead of heading home. We never intended to make our mother worry, we just wanted more time for recess. The time got away from us. Meanwhile, our mother was home watching the clock and after the time passed that we were supposed to be home, she panicked. She paced the floor for about ten minutes before taking my younger brother, John, to my grandparents' house so that she could look for us. Negative thoughts consumed her as she walked the familiar route that she taught us hoping to see us walking home. She called out our names when she approached the playground area. She saw us playing there. I heard her call my name but decided to ignore her. I wanted to play a little while longer it was worth the risk.

"Kalena…. Dwight," she yelled.

When we didn't come to her right away, she hurried over to the playground. Dwight ran to meet her knowing that we were in trouble.

"Get your ass over here," She yelled.

"Mama I'm sorry," Dwight cried out.

I finally ran over to her too but didn't say a word; I wasn't going to make up an excuse. I wasn't sorry about staying after school. She didn't waste any time pulling her belt out of her purse to whip our butts. We thought we were going to get the skin beat off us. She grabbed me by my arm and landed some pretty good licks on my butt. After she finished, she started running after Dwight, but he was bold, he ran from her. When I saw him pick up the pace, I did too. I wanted to catch up to him.

She chased us all the way home while cussing and swinging her belt at the same time. Several on-lookers pulled over to the side of the road and watched in disbelief. She must have looked like a crazed black woman on a mission. Luckily for her, back then parents could whoop their kids without repercussions. Dwight was crying out of fear of getting a whooping, but I wasn't going to give my mother the satisfaction. Showing my emotions to her wasn't an option. I gave myself permission to be stubborn, which made her furious. Whenever she tried to discipline me, she became frustrated because I wouldn't cry. She felt like she was in authority whenever she spanked me, but I felt powerful every time I was able to control my emotions by holding back my tears. My mother didn't realize that my tough exterior resulted from the environment she provided for me and from my need to always be in survival mood.

Being Kalena at school meant being mouthy. I wasn't scared of anybody, and if you backed me up in a corner, you'd find out just how tough I was. Dwight was different, it took a lot to get a rise out of him, but if he got mad enough, he'd come out swinging. School became our sanctuary; being there helped us escape our home life. We'd challenge each other during recess to see who could swing the highest or hang upside down the longest on the monkey bars. I was a tomboy at heart. Dwight and his friends always invited me to play football, basketball, and other sports with them. I could be a bull too and would fight whenever they made me mad. I recall the time Dwight got cornered after school by some boys who always started trouble. They were retaliating against him for things I said earlier that day. I called several of them some bad names for teasing me. Dwight felt like he always had to defend me because of something I said or did. He was noble and did his best to protect me. Although he was terrified of some of them, he would tell anyone who messed with me if they had a problem with me he had a problem with them.

"Leave my sister, Kalena alone," He'd say, but they kept pushing his buttons.

They were relentless, they began calling him names while poking their fingers in his face and weren't going to stop until they provoked him into a fight. He found himself surrounded, but somehow, he was able to break free. He ran home as fast as his feet would allow him to. I tried to divert them by yelling the same nasty names that I did earlier to make them mad in the first place, but they ignored me. It was Dwight's day to get picked on.

It seemed like there was a gang of twenty chasing him, but in reality, it was only ten or twelve boys. I was athletic and could run just as fast as any of the rest of them. I hurried too caught up to Dwight even though he had outrun us. I called his name and tried to get his attention, but he didn't seem to recognize me.

"Dwight, stop we can take these guys," I yelled, but he couldn't hear his mind was affixed on getting home.

I screamed louder, but he still didn't stop. I wanted him to face them, but his fear wouldn't let him. It was like watching a slow-motion movie, where a boy was running in terror, and his sister was running alongside him showing her solidarity. The boys weren't fast enough to catch up to him. When Dwight made it to our house, he hurried up the steps and grabbed the doorknob, but it was locked. It was unusual because my mother always left it unlocked and waited for us to get home from school. Dwight yelled for our mother, but the boy caught up and began pounding him left and right in the back of his head, while he was frantically knocking and pulling on the screen door. When he started to panic so did I, but our grandma Blyler, Frank's mother, opened the door just in time.

"What's all the commotion?" she demanded. The rowdy boy ignored her and kept punching Dwight in the back of his head. "Leave him alone." She yelled. She continued to try to open the screen door to let us in and pleaded with him. "Stop all of this nonsense."

Dwight heard some of the other boys disrespecting our grandma Blyler, and was furious! We were taught to respect our elders at an early age. He wasn't going to allow anyone to talk to our grandmother like that. After grandma Blyler got the screen door open, Dwight who was compiled with fear and anger pushed back within side himself and decided to do something. He started to dash into the house but turned around and all of a sudden, he leaned back and threw a sucker punch that landed straight on the boys' mouth. The other kids gasped and fled to avoid being next. Dwight knocked the boys' front tooth out and busted his lip. It was hilarious to see the boy make a bee-line and run in the opposite direction.

Dwight was out of breath, but he allowed Grandma Blyler to examine his injuries. She explained that our mother had gone to the store and had asked her to let us in when we got home from school.

"Kalena did you see that punch?" Dwight bragged.

"Yep…you busted him right in his lip, that's what he gets for messing with you," I asserted.

Grandma Blyler continues to check him out, but when she attempted to touch his right hand, he screeched.

"Ouch that really hurts," he complained.

"Be still, and let me look,"

Grandma Blyler could tell Dwight was in a lot of pain and believed that he needed to be seen by a doctor. When our mother returned, Grandma Blyler explained to her what happen. Afterward, my mother took Dwight to the hospital emergency room where he was seen.

"You're going to need a cast young man, it looks like you broke it. Can you tell me what happened to your hand?"

"Boy, you wouldn't believe what happened, I busted a boy in the mouth and knocked out his tooth for bullying me." Dwight bragged.

"Well I don't necessarily advocate fighting, but I'd say it looks like you got the better of him." The doctor joked.

"I'm going to have to set your arm in a cast but don't worry you won't have to wear it that long."

Dwight received an additional boost of confidence after his hand was placed in the cast. He bragged about the incident the entire way home. I must admit no one was prouder of him than me. Dwight and I learned a valuable lesson that day. When you face your fears, you earn respect! Dwight had a fan club when he went to school the next day. He had made a name for himself and a reputation for being able to fight. The word at school was if you messed with Dwight Fitzgerald, there would be bloody consequences. His cast became a badge of honor. The boy who he gave the bloody lip avoided both of us like the plague. Everyone asked to sign his cast, and the so-called bullies left both of us alone.

When I was in the fourth grade, I recall having my first crush on a boy named Paul Jenkins. He was a true gentleman. I remember our awkward moments we experienced around each other. I told my Aunt Buttons, Franks' baby sister, about him and she supported my crush. We played together at school whenever we could, and it didn't take too long before he was asking for a kiss. I felt silly, but I wanted to kiss him too. I talked to my Aunt Buttons about it, and she told me that she would help me out.

One day after school Paul invited himself over, he lived across the street from me. We were talking on my front porch and my Aunt Buttons came outside to meet him. I asked her if I could kiss Paul, but he beat me to it by planting a juicy kiss on my lips. We "went together" for a short time after that but our crush fizzled out quickly. Paul was unique, and I was glad that our paths crossed.

Fast forwarding, when Paul turned twenty-one, he died from brain cancer. His parents were Jehovah Witnesses. I was told that they didn't believe in blood transfusions; therefore, he could not undergo the surgery he needed. I do recall how I felt when he died, I had never experienced death before, especially with someone that was close to me. I felt vulnerable and uncertain about the gift of time, at that age you think you will live forever. I couldn't understand for the life of me why his parents didn't allow him to receive the much-needed surgical procedure, regardless of their religious beliefs. Preserving Paul's memory is important to be me because he was my first kiss, and at the time, I believed the death was something that only happened to old people. I thought children were immune to death. If the decision to not have the surgery was because of their beliefs about blood transfusion, Paul's death could've potentially been avoided had his parents made a different decision. In life, there are consequences for everything we do. Some good and some not so good. How many of us have been faced with a situation that didn't appear to provide options for opportunity? Sometimes the answer we need is sitting right there in front of us. The big takeaway for me about Paul's death is people have the power of one's conviction regardless of religion.

Back at home things continued on a downward spiral. My mother and Frank didn't stop verbally abusing us or each other. However, Frank began to show a desire to make a connection with me. He started coming outside to watch my brothers and me play after he got off work. He wanted to make sure that we were safe in our neighborhood. Everyone knew each other, and of course, we were popular since there were so many Fitzgerald's who grew up there. Frank's role in my life as my stepfather earned him some respect, but the truth is he'd never be able to replace the daddy who I longed to know. I never stopped thinking about who he was, or when we would finally meet.

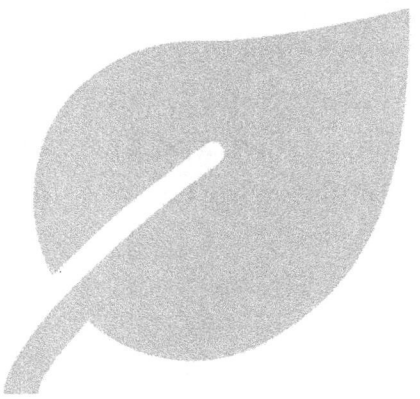

CHAPTER 2

Reflections

My mother would say God awful things to me and later told me that she was attempting to keep us humble, but her negative words and lack of support diminished my self-esteem. Children expect protection from those they look up to and love even if they don't know what that security is supposed to resemble. In my mother's opinion, she was protecting me. I desired my mother's love and wanted to look up to her. Her voice was supposed to be the first one to provide positive building blocks for my self-esteem, but that didn't happen. She was supposed to help define my frame of reference of the world. Some of my first memories of her were of me being verbally abused and belittled. I used my power to help me to recognize that I was somebody and I believed that whole heartily. I developed a force field to protect my heart and mind, but it caused me to become angry deep down inside. That tough exterior wouldn't allow me to shed tears. My mother didn't understand me, which caused a lot of misunderstandings and a lack of trust. It's not a child's responsibility to figure out how you're going to eat or be kept safe.

I acted out by bedwetting until I was about eight years old. It resulted mostly from me being under stress. Being mouthy was another way I protected myself. My natural gifts and abilities weren't being nurtured therefore I became a bully. I chose that avenue to connect to what no one else ununderstood. I sought to defend those who I believed were weak and helpless at times in their lives like my brother, Dwight. Unfortunately, there were no affirmations or positive words told to me by my mother and Frank. They tore me down instead. I protected my heart and mind by building up a tough exterior which helped me to increase my power.

CHAPTER 3

Power of Being Kalena

Do you really believe I didn't know who I was back then? In some ways, you're right because it seemed like the people who mattered the most were the ones who tried their best to deplete my power source, but despite their efforts, I learned how to be courageous. I had to be assertive to protect myself, and even though I wasn't always sure that I was being taken seriously, I didn't stop searching for clues about myself that could help me to become an influential future leader.

Part of that quest to find my truth, I would wrestle with the fact that my mother wasn't willing to help me to connect the dots to ensure that I, her only daughter would grow up with a healthy sense of self-esteem. The truth was that she didn't know how to give that to me. I believe had she gave me what I needed she would have saved us both a lot of anguish and things could've been different for me.

Throughout my adolescence and teen years, my mother repeated the same lies in her effort to conceal information about my daddy. Whenever I asked her who he was, she'd provide vague answers that I could instantly poke holes through. I knew she was telling the truth. I took them with a grain of salt. My sensitivity to the situation made me feel sick to my stomach every time she brought up the subject. She wasn't a person who you'd question without there being repercussions. I always took a page from the notebook of my upbringing "stay in a child's place." However, I remained hopeful and knowing one day I'd find the truth that I was looking for. In some ways, my mother's lies diminished my light; however, my larger than life personality always bounced back and shined a little brighter on my journey to being Kalena which I thanked God for every day.

It was evident that I had a magnetized personality, my mother was reminded whenever she took me out in the community. I recall people approaching her to say, "Oh she's so beautiful," evidence by my brown skin, big brown eyes, and long ponytails but my beauty was something she ignored. She quickly excused herself by being borderline rude, and most of the time she didn't even tell them thank you. I would smile to myself as she would pass others who would repeat the same thing. Most mothers salivated over the compliments others gave them about their children. My mother uses my beauty against me which explains why I hid it until I reached junior high school age.

There were times in my young life when I questioned why my mother was cold and callus. She'd call me nasty names and would force me to answer questions no child my age should have to answer. I cringed every time she asked the one that really bothered me.

"Who do you think you are Mrs. Rich Bitch," she'd say.

Her words cut like a knife causing me to wonder why she despised me so. I felt so sad and alone and would tell myself that when I became a mother, I wouldn't treat my children that way. I'd show them a lot of affection, and say that I love them every day. My mother never had to answer for her bad behavior which was something I didn't understand since we were always surrounded by family. However, she had no idea that God was working on me and was providing me with self-awareness, power, and courage to someday answer her.

My mother wasn't the only person that picked on me and called my integrity into question. Those little elementary school girls wanted to get in on the action. They were the "mean girls" whose actions were like the ones you hear about throughout most schools in America. They were out to get me, and their antics started early because they were jealous of me. Although I can find fault with a lot of things that my mother did to me, I give her credit for making sure that Dwight and I were bathed and dressed in clean clothes. She made sure of that; my hair was always combed and parted neatly down the middle styled into two long ponytails. Back then, if you were a brown-skinned girl with hair that went past your shoulders, you were an automatically targeted and considered a snob. For me, being Kalena meant being feisty enough to keep them at bay but the boys were no different they believed that their job was to tease me and pull my ponytails. They tried really hard to make me cry, but their efforts never worked. They tested my patience daily and learned real fast that I wasn't anybody's crybaby. The mean girls were always yelling out things to hurt my feelings.

"Kalena we're not playing with you today" they'd say.

"Why not," I'd demand.

"Who do you think you are anyway? You think you're better than us just because you've got long hair." The girl with the shortest hair would report.

They assumed that I thought I was better than them, but that wasn't the case, in fact, I figured they were better than me well at least the ones whose mother's drove them to school, or the ones who had their real dad's living in the same. Their rhetoric didn't make any sense. Although I wasn't ready to answer my mother's denigrating question, it was the perfect time to answer the mean girls. I needed to show them my power and that I wasn't afraid. I told myself the next time I was asked: "Who do you think you are?" I was going to produce a powerful response.

I wanted to be ready, I practiced my answer over and over in my head as I walked to school. It seemed they left me alone for a little while to pick on someone else, but I knew they'd be coming for me soon. The bold girl with the short hair began teasing me at recess. I took a deep breath and answered her with all the sassiness that I could muster.

"Who do you think you are?"

"I'm Kalena! How many Kalena's do you know? Being me is something you'll never be!" I felt empowered after answering her. The girl stood there paralyzed with her mouth hanging open. The other's laughed at her and rolled their eyes at me to let me know that my words didn't faze them. Needless to say, those mean girls left me alone after that. I love the fact that the thing my mother gave me that I'm most proud of is my name. Naming me Kalena was a gift that I humbly accepted. My name provides me with a sense of uniqueness, and because of my challenges in life, it was the one thing that helped me to tap into my power along with the ability to stand in the gap for those who were downtrodden like me.

As a young girl, I realized that I was intelligent, and that was something that I wanted people to know, but I spent much of my time managing my relationship with my mother. We continued to struggle because of her lack of support. I wanted her to treat me like I was important especially, but it seemed like my wish was never going to come true.

My mother focused on the things about me that drove her crazy like my defensiveness and smart mouth. I was in survival mode. Whenever she disciplined me, she'd become frustrated when I didn't cry. I refused to and had made up my mind that I wasn't going to give her the benefit of breaking me down. My tough exterior was a result of the environment she created for me, and I displayed it often.

I was my first coaching client although I didn't know that was what I was doing. I filled my mind with positive thoughts and empowering ideas to make it through the day. One thing I told myself was "never allow people to believe they have the upper hand; remain strong so they won't think they have something on you." It was important to me to look brave on the outside even if I was dying on the inside. My self-talk kept me safe and in control over my life. I was providing myself with choices as to how to think and act in situations. Unconsciously, I was unleashing the leader within.

When I was around eleven years old, something happened to me that turned my world upside down. My mind, body, and emotions were going through a transformation. My body began attracting the unwanted attention of men much older than me. My mother taught me early to be cognizance of my surroundings. It wasn't unusual for me to roam freely around my neighborhood. I loved to walk to my grandparent's house and my step-grandparents' house. They all lived relatively close to me. I always had a good time when I went to the Blylers' house. They were Frank's people, and they created a loving atmosphere for everyone. My grandma Blyler was always happy to see my brothers and me. Frank's brothers, sisters, and cousins would also make it even more fun.

One of my favorite things to do on warm summer days was to walk to their house which was by the park. It always felt good to experience the sights, and familiar sounds of families enjoying one another. I'd daydream about my family being able to do the same. I recall walking up 103rd Street toward Flora Park with the warm sun beaming down on my face. As I walked up the street, I noticed the familiar sounds were absent, I couldn't hear any children's laughter, or see any families lying on blankets in the grass enjoying a meal.

Although I found it strange, I kept on walking to my grandparents' house. Out of nowhere appeared a light-skinned black man, who was standing near the edge of a cliff that leads to a steep stairway near the entrance of the park's wooded area. I couldn't tell if he was a teenager or a young man in his early twenties, but I knew he was a lot older than me. I was determined to avoid making eye contact with him since he wasn't someone familiar. I prayed that he wouldn't say or do anything to me as I passed him, but there he stood with his eyes affixed on me. In my spirit, I knew he was up to no good, so I picked up my pace. I was alarmed when he started making catcalls to get my attention.

"Psss…. young thang," he uttered.

I ignored him and kept walking while making sure that I was aware of my surroundings. I looked to my left and then to my right to signal to him that I wasn't afraid of him. I also wanted to send him a message that I wasn't some dumb little girl who didn't know there were men in the world who preyed on girls and boys. I tried to convey that I wasn't nervous, but the faster I walked, the faster he did too causing me some immediate concern.

As I got closer to my grandparent's house, I kept hoping that I would see someone playing in their yard or sitting on the porch like normal. I didn't know if I should run or not, but I was relieved when I noticed Frank's brother, who I called Uncle Jimmy coming out of the house. Uncle Jimmy wasn't someone you'll want to mess with. He was tall and sturdy, and like Frank, he wasn't afraid of anyone since he hung out with blacks and fought a lot when he was younger. He could really hurt someone if he got mad enough. He was coming out of my grandparents' house and was walking towards his vehicle that straddled the sidewalk. When I saw him open his driver's side door, I yelled out his name hoping that the predator would flee.

"Uncle Jimmy," I cried out.

I was relieved when he responded to my voice. He turned around, slammed his car door, and came running towards my direction. I kept yelling frantically.

"Uncle Jimmy help, this man is following me," I shouted.

Uncle Jimmy didn't hesitate to confront the predator. "What do you want? Who are you? What the Fuck are you looking for?" Those were just a few questions that he rattled off. He was furious and was going to do whatever it took to protect me; however, the predator didn't seem to react to his words. He was standing about hundred feet away from him and had a blank stare on his face. The guy was creepy, and it felt like he was looking right through us. I wanted him to challenge Uncle Jimmy so that he could get his tail beat, but he didn't. His lack of response was unusual, but then out of the blue the predator turned around and walked back towards the park.

Uncle Jimmy didn't go after him he grabbed me and hugged me tightly. I was relieved that he was there to run the predator off. Uncle Jimmy didn't call the police, he just stood there holding me.

"Damn girl, I don't know what I would've done if something happened to you." He told me. "Don't tell your mother and Frank. I don't think you'll have to worry about that punk coming back around here."

"Thank you for helping me," I said.

"Kalena, promise me that you'll stay alert. There's a lot of perverts out here."

"I promise to be careful."

I never saw that predator again, but his presence reminded me to always follow my Uncle Jimmy's advice. His willingness to help me solidified the fact that Frank's family loved me even though I wasn't blood and it felt good to know they were in my corner. I continued to visit often. Frank's family taught me that prejudice is something that's learned and not a notion that's rooted in our minds at birth.

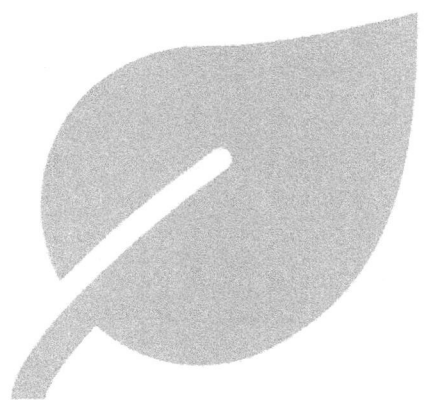

CHAPTER 3

Reflections

The only place I felt rejected was in the home with my mother and Frank. I have a small circle of influence that included my grandparents, aunts, and uncles. Frank's parents were great too; they never shunned us. The outlets outside of my home gave me strength. My Uncle Rod who was married to Frank's sister Beth spent a lot of time with me exploring my creativity by allowing me to participate in outside activities like flying kites and drawing. The contrast between their bi-racial loving relationship and my mother's and Frank was eye-opening. I was able to see and feel love through their relationship. My grandparents loved and protected me, I felt like they always wished and wanted the best for us. What I experienced at home was my "normal," but I knew my grandparents would "do something" if I needed them too. They could be depended upon to come to my rescue. All I had to do was ask! They were the people who showed me unconditional love. I felt safe around them. I didn't want to tell them about the hardships I faced at home. I chose to fill my time with them receiving love and comfort without having to ask for it. The first person who came to my rescue was my brother, Dwight. He was my protector when I wasn't protecting him. He would often try to be a mediator to establish peace in our home. Uncle Rod was a male figure who I saw as a role model. He seemed cool and forward and different from my other uncles. He had a lot of wisdom, and although he was an African American male who became a relative through marriage into Frank's family, he always stood in the gap and kept me safe from Frank's wrath. I was able to suppress the emotions that would heighten my energy around a perceived threat. I believed Frank and my mother wanted to hurt me like I was always somehow at fault. I detach from the current emotional energy of what they wanted me to perceive, feel, and believe. I relied on my power to maintain control. They wanted to shame me by making me cry and to use their words to belittle me. When they told me I couldn't, I told myself I could. I strengthened my ability to be brave. My mama would say she could beat me black and blue and I wouldn't cry. She was right. I maintained a calm and relaxed demeanor when it came to my perceived circumstances. I could make you believe I was disengaged while engaging in the situation to keep myself safe. Frank's sisters and their children gravitated to me. I felt loved and respected by them. Looking back, no one went out of their way to celebrate my birthdays or to give me gifts, each one of them in their own way looked out for me. I told myself that if most of Frank's family accepted me, then he must have as well. The benefit of being around Frank's family gave me the opportunity to be able to live a diverse life that would help me over the course of my lifetime.

CHAPTER 4

Power of Being Beautiful

Changes were happening all around me, and I vowed to seize every moment to take advantage of them. Unbeknownst to me, I was slowly but surely stepping into a higher level of power. Junior High school was a testing ground for that. I knew that I would develop character, and those around me would learn that not only did I have a voice, but I was also willing to use it. I went to Nathan Hale Junior High School, and it was a great experience. I sought to find the answer to the questions about life lessons that most teenagers wanted to know in their informative years, like where do I fit in, will my peers accept me, or which boy would I go with. The answers helped to shape my life experiences.

Living in my own skin was something that came easy for me. I was becoming popular at school and loved to go, and there was so much to learn and do. Looking back, I realize that junior high school years were a place where I could immerse myself in the activities that were offered. I could explore and have the time to imagine what I wanted to be when I grew up. I discovered my strengths and weaknesses. One of which, was the ability to type. I surprised myself by catching on quickly to type 120 wpm. I didn't realize that it would be a skill that I could store in my toolbox for future use. My mind was open to new ideas, and I was impressionable. I recall a teacher name Ms. Black, who was part of the Black Power Movement which started in the early 1950's. Their purpose was to patrol African American neighborhoods to protect the residents from police brutality which is still an issue today. Ms. Black was a strong black woman with distinctive features who dressed mostly in black clothing and wore an enormous afro. She was unapologetic and had a profound effect on me. When she talked, I hung on her every word. She spoke with such vigor to our class that was filled with African American boys and girls who looked like me. It felt good to be black in America when she described our history and how the Black Panthers fought to preserve it. She taught us the familiar chant coined by them "I'm black, and I'm proud." We'd chant those words while pumping our fist in the air. I recall how those words rolled off my tongue with ease. Having that experience allowed me to be a participant and not an observer in a movement that meant a lot to me and others. It was my first taste of leadership from grassroots initiatives in the community, something that I would often do in my life.

I continued to be a sponge as I experience the world through my junior high school lenses. Dwight and I were able to share some of the same experiences, and we remained close confidants as we made new connections and formed our own independence.

The breakdancing craze was taking over most American cities; a lot of the boys in my neighborhood jumped on the bandwagon. Being a breakdancer meant that you were a walking billboard of coolness. There wasn't a lot of girls that could breakdance, but I wanted to be part of the craze. I was a tomboy at heart and believed that I could break the glass ceiling. It was going to be another accolade that I could add to my leadership list. I hung out with my friend Doug, and some other boys that went to my school, they were the best of the best when it came to breakdancing. I became a quick study and was intrigued every time I saw them pull out their cardboard mats to bust a move with ease.

When I showed them the moves I learned on my own, they couldn't believe my swagger and fancy footwork. I could do their most difficult stunts, so they decided to teach me more. I perfected several complicated moves. My favorite was "the windmill," it became one of my signature moves. The news about my abilities spread quickly throughout various neighborhoods. I hoped I was good enough to be recruited by a crew and that my swagger, confidence, and gender would help me to get in. The manager of one of the more popular crews called the Break City Dancers reached out to me. He wanted to talk about the possibility of me joining his team. He told me that I was the missing link and asked me if I would join. I was thrilled and said that he had to talk to my mother and Frank first. He didn't waste any time calling them to ask for permission.

"Ms. Fitzgerald, your daughter is a good breakdancer. We could use somebody like her in our crew. Would you let her join?" he asked.

"I don't mind she's always doing those dangerous tricks around the house. I tell her to go outside all the time. It might do her some good," my mother told him.

I was surprised that my mother agreed to let me join. We practiced every day, but I didn't allow it to affect my grades at school. We performed a lot in our neighborhood, and our popularity grew. The crowd was hype whenever we did our flashy moves, but when I did my solo, they went berserk. I had a lot to prove since I was a girl even though I was comfortable in my own skin. I added several more moves to my arsenal that included variations of the Head Spin, the Worm, and the Helicopter and became a crowd favorite. My crew loved having me, and they were ecstatic that we had the secret weapon over other crews.

"Kalena you're so dope! We gonna call you "Special K." They told me.

"Special K?" I replied.

"Hell yeah, you're the shit."

Some of the other crews were jealous because I was part of the Break City Dancers and we got paid for our gigs. Our manager was able to negotiate more money for me because I was a girl. I received fifty dollars for each show, while the other members got twenty-five dollars. It was my first taste of entrepreneurship, and it felt electrifying! I worked hard to bolster my reputation as a breakdancer and to live up to my name "Special K." I had the look of a breakdancer too and went to great lengths to fit the stereotype. I took the money I earned and bought Bboy clothes and accessories to look the part. I had headbands, bandannas, wristbands, baggy shirts, knee pads, and a few pairs of fresh sneakers. My shoe game was on point. I had PUMAS and ADIDAS, which were the shoes to have if you were a legit breakdancer. When I wore my Bboy outfits, I looked dope and felt powerful.

Being part of something bigger than myself provided me with a much-needed layer of self-esteem. I began connecting more dots about my identity through my breakdancing experience. I was no different than my male crew members with their huge egos. Mine was bigger than theirs at times especially when I busted a move, and the crowd went crazy for me. The ability to breakdance was yet another gift God gave me, and I believe that He wanted me to realize my greatness and to be able to draw from it.

Looking back, even though I loved breakdancing and hanging out with my crew it didn't help me to embrace my feminine side. In fact, if I had it my way I would've breakdanced with my crew forever. They made me feel a true sense of belonging and oneness. They understood things about me that others didn't. Hanging around them allowed me to escape my home life too. However, my breakdancing days were slowly coming to an end.

God places people in our lives whose job is to take us to a higher state of being. Their purpose is to help us reconcile the internal conflicts we face when it comes to making tough decisions about which road to take or they help sort things out when we're unsure if we're doing what's right at any given time. For me, that person was my neighbor Dough Freeman, AKA Douggie. He was a few years older than me, but he was someone who was respected by everyone in the neighborhood. He'd watch my crew practice in the backyard, and I recall him asking if he could talk to me after practice one day. I noticed him sitting on his front porch, but on this particular day, his eyes were affixed on me. He wanted to tell me something about myself that I should've already known and when he spoke his words caused me to view the world through a different pair of lenses.

"Kalena, come here," he demanded. I didn't hesitate to run over to see what he wanted. "Let me see those wristbands and that headband you're wearing." He said.

"Okay, I guess you can look at them, but I need them back," I said even though I didn't know why he wanted to see them. Maybe he wanted some for himself, and he desired look at mine.

I observed him carefully as he examined them. He sized me up and down then continued studying them.

"I don't want to see you dressed like this again. You're too pretty to be hiding behind these props" he warned.

My feelings were instantly hurt. Douggie's comments threw me for a loop. No one had ever told me what I was doing was inappropriate. I dropped my head down in shame and felt embarrassed. I was perplexed up to that point, I had believed in what my crew was doing. We were entertainers and whose goal was to do something positive in the community. Douggie was insinuating me, my gut reaction was to challenge him, but I didn't have the nerve since he was older than me. At that moment, I considered whether it was time to stop acting like a boy or if I should begin focusing on my outer beauty. I wanted to ignore Douggie altogether because I loved to breakdance. I never wanted to be just another pretty face in the crowd, but Douggie's words had taken hold of me, and I wanted to change my outlook on life at that time to step into my power.

Douggie's was right; I had been hiding behind my baggy Bboy clothes on purpose and hanging out with my crew instead of dressing up and hanging out with other girls my age. My actions were overshadowing my beauty, and it was time for a change. I took his advice after considering how my beauty could benefit me. I recalled seeing the Barbizon School of Modeling in downtown Cleveland. I wondered what it would be like to take a few lessons, but I never acted on my inquiry.

My relationship with my mother had begun to improve after she supported me by allowing me to breakdance. She found time in her day to talk to me about things that mattered to me, and I began trusting her with my feelings. I decided to share with her my desire to take some classes at Barbizon. She offered to help by making some calls to inquire about how much it would cost. She provided me with the information once she called and reminded me that we couldn't afford it. She suggested that I ask my grandparents for help and gave me her blessing to do so. My grandparents had always done their best to help me, but I didn't want to ask because I knew they didn't have extra money.

My mother encouraged me to follow my dreams but insisted that I make sure that modeling was something I really wanted to do before asking my grandparents for the money. I took about a week to think about it and questioned myself about how modeling was going to benefit me or if I would actually stick with it since I hadn't been into the girly stuff much lately. Looking back, I books on my head. I mastered the lesson and realized that it was a powerful one. My grandparents taught the lesson of grace a little differently, to them the lesson of grace meant having an awareness that people struggle in life and it's our responsibility to support them. It's not our job to subject them to harsh criticism like most people do in the world. Both lessons resonated with me and I began to intertwine them. I wanted a measure of grace to be given to me based on the circumstances I faced in my life.

I learned a lot more important lessons at Barbizon which prepared me for a bigger platform. When I finished my classes, my mother and grandparents were proud of me, and I was ready to move on to the next chapter in my life. I decided that would be competing in a beauty pageant. I wanted to stretch myself, so I entered a local beauty pageant in Cleveland. Most of the young ladies who participated were experienced and had competed in pageants for years. Did it feel awkward? Yes, it did! Was I nervous, scared? Absolutely! These girls were professionals, and I truly admired their confidence and I wanted mine. I believed that being involved in a pageant would be a testing ground to apply all the life's lessons I had learned thus far. I found that I could adapt to whatever circumstances came my way. It was a truth that I had forgotten. I was now a confident, poised, powerful, and young lady and wanted badly to take home the crown.

Surprisingly my mother continued to support me. She had started to find her own way and depended less on Frank. I was proud of her and happy that she was making herself available to me. She took me shopping for my first pageant dress. I recall the fun we had shopping. I couldn't believe how much was changing and I welcomed her loving demeanor. That day we went to a lot of stores to find the perfect dress. I settled on a bright yellow one with a lot of ruffles. The store clerk said it was a typical pageant dress. The night of the pageant, I sized up the competition told myself I was going to be a front-runner even though it was my first pageant. I was ready to accept the crown.

I walked confidentially into the pageant hall and noticed right away the young lady who I believed was my biggest competition who was wearing an elegant evening gown. I felt embarrassed after realizing that I had a lot to learn about pageants. My heart sank in my chest, and I hurried into the bathroom to avoid being seen. I hid out in there as long as I could until I heard the announcer instructed us to get in the lineup to go on stage. When I heard him call my name, I paraded onto the stage hoping the audience would focus on my beauty and intellect, not my bulky little house on the prairie yellow ball gown. It was apparent that I was wearing the wrong dress, but the judges accepted me without prejudice. When you're a tomboy turned princess, I had a few challenges figuring this thing out! I learned that night that in life things aren't always going to be perfect, and at times embarrassing, so you must embrace every situation knowing you should do your best. Although I was competitive in the interviewing phase of the competition, I placed fifth overall. I was disappointed that I didn't win, but I felt grateful for the opportunity.

The thought of being preyed on for the second time really upset me because I didn't think it could happen twice in a million years but it did. It was like Déjà vu. As a young girl, I couldn't wrap my mind around why I seemed to be a target for predators. On the day in question, I headed out for school like I did most mornings, but before I could make it up the street a few blocks, I noticed a yellow beetle bug, which was a popular vehicle made by Volkswagen sitting on the side of the road. It looked out of place and caused me some concern. I wondered who it belonged to since I lived in a close-knit neighborhood and most of my neighbor's vehicles were familiar to me.

As I passed the car, I noticed that a younger white man was sitting inside who didn't look familiar. I immediately felt sick to my stomach, and I thought to myself "here's another predator lurking around how am I going to get away." I tried hard to avoid eye contact with him and to take inventory of my surroundings casually looking to my right and left. I expected to hear him getting out and coming after me, but I didn't. I was relieved that I wasn't his target.

I breathed a sigh of relief once I reached the school property, but continue to feel uneasy throughout the rest of the day and found it difficult to focus. On the way home, I surveyed the area to make sure the yellow beetle bug wasn't around. I didn't see it, so I felt safe enough to walk home. Dwight and I usually walked back and forth to school together, but he had become frustrated with me because I was acting "like a girl" and he wanted his tomboy sister back.

When I got home, I decided not to tell my mother and Frank. I didn't want to make them upset. I figured it was merely a coincidence. I walked to school cautiously the next day; however, I noticed that the yellow beetle bug was parked in the same location again. Alarms went off in my head, and I saw flashing lights cautioning me that "Stranger Danger" was looming. I was terrified and knew the predator was up to no good. I decided I needed to take a different route so I wouldn't have to walk by the predator's car. The next day, I noticed that the strange man had parked in a new location, he parked his car on the same side of the street that I was walking on. I told myself that I was going to get abducted, I'm being stalked! Right before passing his car I made a beeline right and turned down one of the side streets to take a different route to school. My heart was pumping out of my chest and I was hoping that he wouldn't follow me.

After the third sighting, I decided to tell my mother and Frank when I got home from school. Frank told me to take the back roads that would cause me to walk in the opposite direction taking a lot longer to get to school. I was worried the predator would drive around my neighborhood looking for me when I wasn't where he expected me to be.

"Mama, there's been a strange white man hanging around, I saw him sitting in his car three days in a row," I reported.

"Did he say anything to you?" Frank demanded.

"No, I went down 105th street to get away from him,"

"Kalena, I want you to take a different route tomorrow. Don't go down Etna Street, take the back way."

Frank assured me that he was going to check things out the next morning prior to me leaving the house to walk to school. When I got up he was gone, he had woken up early to drive his car up the street and around the corner to look for the stranger as promised. Frank found him and parked his car close by to observe him. He wanted to see how long the predator was going to loiter around in the neighborhood and figured since I was a young black girl, the predator wouldn't be able to detect that Frank being a white man was there on my behalf or that we were related. After watching him for what seemed like a few minutes, Frank decided to confront him. He pulled his car up to the vehicle and jumped out of his car and slammed the door to alert the predator. He wasn't welcome in our neighborhood and certainly wasn't welcome to his daughter. The predator sat there in his vehicle with his windows rolled up trying to look oblivious to Frank. He was looking for a new victim. Frank approached the driver's side door and began firing off a series of questions.

"Who are you and what do you want with my daughter?" Frank asserted. The predator didn't say a word instead he started up his vehicle and sped off. Frank hurried back to his car to chase him. The chase lasted twenty minutes down a busy city street that led to the freeway on 55th. Unfortunately, the predator got away. Frank called the police and reported the incident.

"911 what's your emergency?"

"I want to report a strange white man who's been lurking around my neighborhood, and he's been preying on my daughter."

"What did he look like and did you get his license plate number?"

"I sure did, it's 449JTY, he was white and looked to be between thirty or forty," Frank told them.

After running the predator's license plate, the police reported that the man lived in Solon, which is a nearby city located thirty miles away from our community by freeway. The police told Frank there was no rhyme or reason why he was there, and they would keep an eye out for him. It was apparent that the predator had an agenda, and it was to abduct me, but by the grace of God, his plans were foiled.

CHAPTER 4

Reflections

I wanted to appeal to boys. I saw the girls that they were attracted to and wanted to look pretty just like them, but there were limits to how far I would go. My look was changing once I began to press my hair and to wear make-up. I wanted to feel pretty and to be appealing. I wanted the boys to like me, at least the ones I liked. Dwight needed to understand that I was changing and that my hormones were raging! We were moving in different directions. By the time I got to high school; we had enrolled in different schools which forced us to find our own way. I felt like being beautiful in other's people's eyes was a distraction. I still wanted to be taken seriously when it came to intelligence. I didn't want to be any one's primp and perfect beauty queen that sat on church pew without a voice. My vision for my life was to be a roaring lion. My goal was to carry myself with poise and confidence. Having Frank come to my rescue after being prey on felt good. He was at times "my hero." But here's the deal, looking back, Frank only had a fourth-grade education, and the choices he made had nothing to do with me. His fear, abuse, control, and anger belonged to him. I also knew my mother choices were hers as well. I decided that their reality wasn't going to be mine. Frank always made sure we had a roof over our heads and food on the table. He was doing his personal best with what he felt he had to work with. My mother's perceptions and beliefs on how to keep me safe and humbled had nothing to do with me. She was acting on her own fears and reality. Their views and parenting styles were "all kinds of crazy" but they did what they thought was best, and I can respect that, but it doesn't mean I have to accept that. Being a prey twice at that age made me feel at risk. I felt vulnerable. Walking was something I had to do, and I realized that it could be compromised at any time. For two years after I graduated high school on my way to work every day, I would have to walk about a half a mile to get to the bus stop, I carried a big stick and hid it in the bushes just in case. It was a huge monkey stick that had a calling card attached to it...mess with me and see what will happen to you! However, I was too embarrassed to carry it on the bus with me, so I placed it in the bushes. I was a tough girl, and tough girls didn't look scared. I realized early on that having a pretty face had a price; it caused me to have an increased sense of awareness. I received validation that I was good at something when my mother allowed me to be in the Break City Dancers. It was something everyone in our family could celebrate since my brothers were also breakdancers. Living in my own skin meant I needed to reframe some things in life and give them a new purpose. I learned to use fear as an advantage. It was difficult at times to meet my own expectations. I always defaulted to emotional intelligence when life threw a curve. Life can send you through some difficult times that can be detrimental. The question is how will we use our story to impact others? I also wanted to live a life in which others knew I was here. My mantra is "I WAS HERE!" When I need inspiration, I listen to Beyoncé's song with the same name to lift me up and to kick start my dreams. My high school provided me with a thirst to be an advocate for others; my biggest dream back then was to become an attorney. I take pride in the fact that I never drummed to the beat of others and have always been a leader. I stood up for the things I believed in. As a young adult, I often in my dreams saw myself speaking to large crowds with power and conviction. I was winning popularity contests at school and could influence others. As a Christian, I felt like I represented hope for others my age.

CHAPTER 5

Power of Finding my Daddy

I was on a quest to seek the truth about my daddy, but my mother had her own ideas about what she thought I needed to know. When I was around thirteen, I asked her who he was although I feared the repercussions. I had the right to know. I was once again taking a small step towards using my power, by having the courage to ask the questions that would help me learn more about my identity.

My mother wasn't ready to reveal the truth and decided to continue her sham. She told a lie so big that it would eventually backfire on her one day. She made up a fictitious person who I'll refer to as Michael Davis. She told me that he was my daddy and she was willing to help me find him.

"Kalena, your father's is Michael Davis," my mother asserted while providing with a few vague details about him.

As I listened to the description that she provided, I closed my eyes to allow my imagination to visualize what my perfect daddy looked like and the day we'd get a chance to meet.

"Momma can we look for him," I asked as my eyes widen with excitement.

"Yes, we can try, but I'm not sure where he's living right now. We can go to the house where he used to live, but I can't promise anything," she told me.

I was ecstatic! I couldn't wait to look for him, but I didn't know what I'd say if we found him. After we drove across town and arrived at our destination, my mother nervously walked up to the house where she said he lived. She knocked on the door, and when an older man opened it, she asked if my daddy was there.

"Hello, I was wondering if Michael Davis still lives here?"

"Ma'am, no one by that name lives here." He told her.

I didn't understand why my mother would take me to a house where she knew my daddy didn't live. She looked puzzled and said that she thought he might have moved. She said we could go to another house where he may have moved to. It felt like we were searching for a ghost. After she got tired of her charade, she told me that it was possible that my daddy left the area. She said she heard that he moved somewhere near St. Clair street, which was a neighborhood notorious for danger. I wasn't going anywhere near that part of town. I gave my mother some credit that day, the charade helped me to remain hopeful about meeting my daddy; but I knew deep down inside that there was something erroneous happening and I would have been content for the next few years.

I continued to thrive in junior high and cemented my relationship with good friends and did well academically. One such friend was Kimberly Smith; we became best friends in elementary school. She and I walked to school together every day and shared secrets. We learned how to do sign language together. We communicated in a way that most of the people couldn't. We would pass one another in the hallway and would sign our thoughts then we'd bust out into laughter.

We studied together, and whenever we were in the same class, we cheated on tests by signing but never got caught. I recall having surgery on my feet when I was twelve, and Kimberly was there for me. She took it upon herself to make sure I got all the homework that was issued. There were times she even completed it herself and turned it in for me. Our bond never wavered.

My cousin Kimberly even though we lived together babies had not hung out together as teenagers that much but one summer our parents send us off to camp. When I was with her, we'd act silly without apologizes. The camp staff encouraged everyone to participate in a talent show on the last night. I was never shy as a child. I decided to showcase my talent by singing "I Believe the Children Are Our Future." I thought I sound pretty good and had plenty of practice singing it in the shower. I took a few minutes to practice prior to going on stage, and but had to go to the bathroom, while in there I noticed that I had started my period and didn't have any supplies. I attempted to hold off the bleeding by putting some toilet paper in my panties prior to walking out of the bathroom. Unbeknown to me, I left a long piece hanging out of my shorts. When I walk on the stage, the kids burst into laughter as they were pointing to my shorts. I looked down to examine myself and found the source of their laughter. I was embarrassed but laughed at myself too and finished my performance despite my situation. That is a memory I'll never forget it still amuses me today.

CHAPTER 5

Reflection

In not having my daddy around fueled my vision of a man who I knew would someday be proud of me. Not having a visualization image of him, forced me to create a dialogue in my mind about the things he would say to me to let me know that he was proud of me. Although my daddy was invisible, I created him in the image God gave me for him. His persona became larger than life itself. I permitted myself to create in my environment the person I wanted to be. The power inside of me took on contributing factors of what I felt I would gain from his invisible DNA. I thought I looked different and I felt different. I knew my daddy had something to do with my intelligence, beauty, and my aggressive nature. I felt like my life had taken me to a lot of different places because my family moved around a lot. I believed it was possible that my daddy was looking for me too and I always knew we'd meet. When my mother suggested we look for him to clear her conscious, I was thrilled knowing he would no longer be invisible. I would finally be able to see, hear, smell, and touch him. Growing up, I never asked my mother much about him. I figured I'd know him when I saw him since my mother wasn't capable of impregnating herself. I rationalized our looking for him as a good sign that he and I would eventually meet somewhere in the middle. I don't hold any grudges or unforgiveness against my mother or anyone else. My struggles without my daddy helped to sharpen my saw and gave me the strength I needed to persevere. If my daddy had been a part of my life, it would've turned out different, and I wouldn't be able to tell my powerful story of and resilience that has become my testimony to other women who have experienced a life similar to mine.

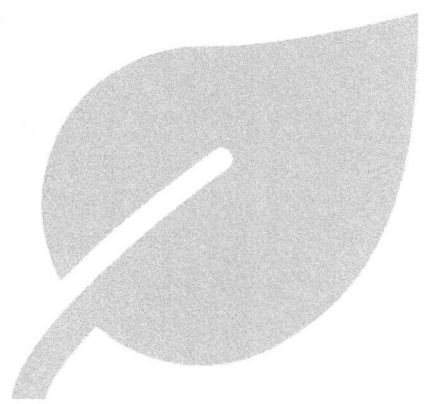

CHAPTER 6

Power of Protecting my Mother

Transitioning to high school was an exciting time for me especially given the fact that I would be attending Law & Public Service Magnetic High School located on 71st and Hough. I was ready to embrace its rich tradition and to be a part of the school's sorority Alpha Phi Angels' which was an extension of Cleveland State College Alpha Phi Alpha's. It gave me an opportunity to see the world through other young lady's vantage points, and I learned from some of their experiences.

Every time I stepped on campus, I felt a surge of power and quickly realized that my life would never be the same.

It didn't take long for me to find my voice and to express myself outwardly. I began to allow my clothing to define me and loved dressing up. I actually became strategic about the outfits I wore. I'd drape myself in layered gold necklaces that were different lengths and styles they gave me a sense of sophistication. Owning a real gold chain back then was a big deal and status symbol. I was attempting to find the uniqueness in myself that no one else recognized about me and it was working. People began taking me seriously, and it felt good.

I got a job at Kenny Kings one summer, a chicken outfit located in the Parma Mall in Cleveland. Dwight worked there too, he was able to help me get the job. I loved the benefit of having a free meal which we earned before or after our working shift. I loved their fried chicken; it was some of the best in town. I used most of my paycheck to purchase clothes since looking nice every day had become a priority.

I got connected right away and began to participate in extra curriculum activities. I played basketball, but volleyball was my favorite. My transformation caught the attention of some of the young men at my school. However, there was one guy in particular that caught my attention; his name was Shank. He was a popular junior who was tall dark and handsome. I felt lucky to have his attention since I was just a freshman. Shank was easy on the eyes and lot of girls liked him too.

I recall the night I met him; it was at a school dance. I was watching him from afar and admiring the way he danced. I wanted him to notice me, and he eventually did. A slow song stared to play, I decided to go up to him and ask if he wanted to dance? He said he was a little sweaty, I piped right up and said, "I don't mind a little sweat." That song felt like it went on forever. While dancing I allowed him to see how much I really liked him by snuggling into him as the song played. Later that night he approached me to ask for my telephone number I was nervous. My underarms were sweating, but I didn't hesitate to give it to him. I wished he'd use it to call me right away although I knew it would be difficult for him to reach me. Things were complicated back then with those old school telephones. It would be anyone's guess when we would be a chance to talk. I didn't have the liberty of talking to Shank for hours that was something my mother wouldn't allow. Dwight was also interested in the girls, and he was getting more than his fair share of telephone calls. Shank took his sweet time to call me, but I knew that he was interested in me by the way he checked me out whenever I passed him in the hallway at school.

I found out from a friend that he was dating a pretty girl, so I assumed that was the reason he hadn't called. I didn't want Shank to get away. I made a point to make sure he saw me every day. I was quickly becoming one of the popular pretty girls at school, and a lot of the boys were interested in me. However, my sights were squarely set on Shank. When he finally called, it didn't take long to realize that we had a lot in common. He eventually broke up with his girlfriend, and we became an item.

Walking around the school on Shank's arm was a big deal. Most of my friends were happy for me, but there were some who wanted him themselves and were bold enough to let me know. Shank was experienced and was already having sex. I was still a virgin and wanted to take things slow. He promised me that we would and said he would never expect me to do anything that I wasn't comfortable with. The first time Shank kissed me, my knees buckled underneath me and I knew he was the one.

Shank couldn't keep his hands to himself; they were all over me every time we were together. I was happy to tell my mother about him, but she warned me that most upperclassmen wanted to take advantage of the incoming freshman girls and to be careful. She didn't want me to repeat any of her mistakes.

"Kalena, you have to watch those older boys they just want to get in your pants,"

"Mama Shank is different," I said lacking the wisdom she had,

"Besides I already told him that I'm a virgin and we should take things slow because I'm not ready to have sex with anyone," I said.

"It's not you who I don't trust," she joked.

I wanted my mother to meet Shank so I could prove her wrong. I thought my judgment was just as good as hers but also knew that she was right. A lot of my close friends were complaining about their boyfriends pressuring them to have sex. I thought Shank was different and prayed that he wouldn't dare take my innocence. I invited him over one day and asked my mother to come into the living to meet my tall chocolate dark handsome boyfriend. Mid-way through the introductions, I blurted out "This is Shank and no mama he hasn't asked me to have sex with him." I'm not sure why I was bold enough to tell her that at that moment, but I'm sure Shank was embarrassed. My mother gave me one of her familiar looks that meant sooner or later I'd be apologizing to her for being wrong, but I pretended not to notice. Luckily for me, she thought Shank was a nice and considerate young man.

I tried to balance my crush on Shank with my desire to excel in school. I also worked at the YMCA and participated in a program that required me to travel to the capital of Ohio to learn and take part in a mock scenario of how the legislative process worked. We were given specific roles to advocate for the necessity of having a living will. We had to argue for both sides reflecting the Democratic process. Of course, I took my role seriously and was able to demonstrate my ability to argue for the side I agreed with. I was the perfect mouthpiece to champion for our team. I learned a lot about myself and my ability to vocalize and champion for causes really surprised me. I found out that I could be the voice for others when they needed one.

Things became serious between Shank and me. We were inseparable, and it seemed like nothing could come between us. I belonged to him, and all the boys knew Shank would come after them if they tried to talk to me. He warned them to keep their distance. I pretended to have the perfect home life and could escape the uncertainty of it when I was at school and by turning my attention to the opposite sex.

Shank was slowly winning me over. He was grooming me to have sex with him, and I didn't know it. And when he thought I wanted him bad enough to go all the way, he gently guided me there. I remember our first time, I didn't know what I was doing, but it felt right. He was gentle with me. We started having sex whenever or wherever we could. I found out that I was pregnant during my sophomore year, something I thought would never happen. Shank and I had failed to use protection and were now faced with a new set of consequences. Shank had already graduated from high school and joined the military. We were still a couple, and I talked to him while he was away. My mother made it possible for us to communicate by allowing him to call our house collect a few times a month.

I was nervous to tell him about the baby, but Shank seemed to believe that it was a good idea to have it but I didn't feel the same way. I wasn't ready to give up my power to become a teen mom. Shank asked me to go to his mama's house to make it easier on me to keep our baby. I'm not sure how he thought that was going to happen I couldn't leave my mother's house without there being problems. I finally got the courage to tell my mother about being pregnant. Although she was upset, she helped me to make the arrangements to have an abortion. I had two options leave or abort the baby. My mother made it clear that aborting the baby was my only option. It must have seemed like Deja vu for her when she found out since she had found herself in the same situation while in high school. Needless to say, I had the abortion. Later that year, I discovered Shank was dating another girl behind my back too. I was furious! His bad behavior helped me to realize that I made the right choice by ending our relationship. The decision to terminate my pregnancy was a heart-wrenching decision that I would never fully get over.

The following school year, I decided to run for Junior Class President and won! My school life was going well, and I got a part-time job at Rainbow Fashions located in Downtown Cleveland on 4th street, which lasted for three years. I loved working there because it fueled my desire to look pretty and dress up all the time. I spend my entire paycheck on clothes. Working at Rainbow allowed me the opportunity to help my mom with school clothes for my brothers as well.

My home life was an entirely different story. My mother and Frank's relationship hit the rocks after he returned home from a weekend fishing trip to deliver my mother the worst news of her life. It seemed like yesterday. I was on the front porch when Frank blew passed me to get inside the house. He had been gone all weekend. He slammed the screen door behind him causing me some concern. He and my mother began arguing, and I could hear what they were arguing about. Frank told my mother that he was going to leave her for another woman. Until that point, I thought my mother was strong and capable of defending herself as she had so many other times when they had gotten into a fight.

I could hear my mother's heartbreak, a sound that thundered like a stormy night, and I knew she would never be the same. I listened in disbelief to her sobbing something I never heard her do in such a way. Her pain was deep, and she pulled it up from the pit of her belly while rocking herself back and forth on the floor. I peeked through the screen door to see if I could help, but I couldn't in that moment, we were both helpless. My mother was facing her worst fears and everything that weighed on her as a young girl was coming back to haunt her, like past insecurities, and feelings of unworthiness. I had never seen anyone in pain like that before, and she scratched at the air while screaming loudly. There was an eeriness, which resulted from Frank's admission of infidelity.

Frank left my mother and my brothers, but they were willing to forgive him for his transgressions. My power kicked in, and I felt like I was the only person in our house capable of making decisions, willing to fight, get help, and maintain order. I took on the role as protector and the power within allowed me to do it. I decided to step down from my role as Junior Class President to make myself available in case Frank came back home wanting to fight. I realized that I couldn't do anything sitting in a classroom way across town and if something were to happen, it would take forever to get home since I rode two buses to school. I thought by the time I got home she could've been injured badly or worse dead. I carried her weight on my seventeen-year-old shoulders and vowed to fight Frank if necessary. I wanted a moment to come head to head with him for inflicting pain and agony in the lives of the people I loved.

We remained close with Frank's family, and my Grandma Blyler invited us over for Christmas. I recall having to walk there since we didn't have a vehicle. Frank took it too. My mother didn't expect him to be there and thought he would be embarrassed to show his face since by then everyone knew their situation. Grandma Blyler had prepared a feast, and when we arrive, she announced it was time to eat. However, when we sat down at the table, we heard a knock at the door. Uncle Rod excused himself to answer it. When he came back, in walked Frank with him behind him, and it was obvious that he'd been drinking, his eyes were blood-shot red. I wanted to jump from the table to fight him right then and there and couldn't believe that he would show up and ruin his family's Christmas dinner. My mother tried to ignore him, but he began making a scene in front of everyone.

"I need to talk to you woman," he announced followed by "Why have you been avoiding me?"

My mother didn't answer him she didn't want to ruin the family dinner. She politely excused herself and walked toward the back door to go outside on the back porch. Frank followed her and slammed the door. We could hear their argument from behind closed door, and what sounded like my mother being shoved up against the house. She was crying which made me ever madder. I begged my Uncle Rod to intervene by opening the door, but he asked if she open it. I said "yes, open the door!" In that moment anger rose up on the inside of me. It felt like a burst of power, the kind Wonder Woman gets before going into action, and I busted through the door to help my mother.

"Get off my mother motherfucker," I yelled out as I saw Frank who had my mother pinned up against the house with a knife at her throat. Frank lunged for me and when he did, Uncle Rod grabbed him and demanding that he leave. I blacked out for a moment, all I could see was red, but I could hear Uncle Rod's voice of reason.

"Frank…Frank…Frank, you don't want to do this. Just leave," he told him.

Uncle Rod had no other choice but to throw Frank out because he didn't get it and wouldn't stop. Needless to say, he did ruin our Christmas dinner, but we tried to make the best out of a bad situation. Uncle Rod took us home since we lived down the street and around the corner from my Grandma Blyler's house; came in and stayed for a little while to make sure we were safe.

CHAPTER 6

Reflection

Looking back now, I don't know if it was anxiety or the shame or perceived fear of being rejected by my family for becoming pregnant. So much so, that I didn't even begin to realize that it was the life of a child that I aborted. Through the years, I have often tried to calculate the age my child and wanted to know if it was a boy or a girl. I envision it was a boy. I have even wondered what life with a thirty-year-old would have been like. My decisions were made for me at the time, and I had no power. I wish I could've utilized a wider range of possibilities and opportunities in my decision-making. When I think about my loss, a sense of sadness, hidden regret, feelings of wonder and "what if" comes over me. There are things that I will never know. Even though there is this great sadness, I won't allow my past to dictate a negative future. It's up to me on how I show up in this world regardless of my past or current circumstances. I refuse to be a victim, I'm victorious. A wise man said that life doesn't offer us problems or challenges, only opportunities. The abortion is probably one of the reasons why I'm an advocate for women and why I devote my life to help them. It's an honor and a privilege that I get the opportunity to guide them and encourage them. I empathize with those going through the same thing I did. Other people gave me permission to have courage, and to know that I'm not crazy for exerting my power by being strong for others. I learned that I was capable of weathering the aggressive storms of life. There wasn't anything that I didn't feel I couldn't do. I felt like I had the strength of a thousand oak trees when it came to my brothers and mother. Being strong at that time also fed my ego. I've since turned it around, as an adult being strong and protecting others translates into self-preservation. I show other women how to show up and to have a voice through our sisterhood. Standing up for my mother came naturally. It was instinct, and I was the only one who could protect her at the time. My mother had been abused by a vindictive man who I didn't like. My mother was hurting, and I had compassion and empathy for her. Having to relinquish my responsibilities as the Junior Class President didn't matter I chose to put her first even though the same hadn't been done for me. I viewed myself as the stronger one who had the power to protect those who couldn't protect themselves and my mother fit that category.

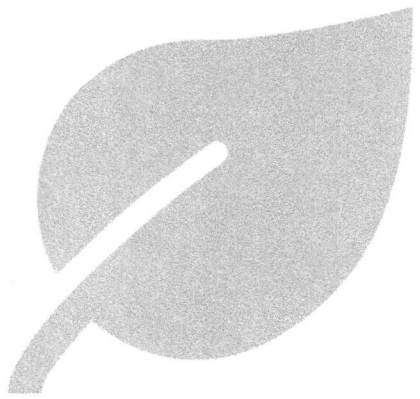

CHAPTER 7

Power of Forgiveness

Elaine was my mother's best friend and a fixture in our home for as long as I could remember. I really liked her, and she seems to bring out the best in my mother. My mother was carefree in her presence, and there was a lot of laughter between the two of them. I didn't know why, but Elaine was protective of me. I heard her tease my mother often for having a crush on her brother, Larry. She had always thought that I could be his daughter.

I remained consumed with thoughts about my daddy and wondered where he was and what he looked like. I knew that I'd get to meet him someday and I wasn't going to let my mother's inability, to tell the truth, to stop me. My mother and Elaine could be heard whispering whenever I was in the same room with them. They filled the air with innuendos about my mother's past. I'd ease drop to hear bits and pieces of the puzzle, but it is hard to solve with the tidbits of info I heard. In my gut, I believed that the information they whispered about had something to do with me.

When I was seventeen, I recall sitting in our living room looking at some photos of myself. They varied from the early years of my life to my high school days. I found my journey to becoming a young lady amusing. As a family, we took a lot of pictures, and there were plenty of memories preserved in our photo albums. Elaine was over, and when she noticed me looking at pictures, she came over and said she wanted to join me. We laughed at the funny ones that were captured at my grandparents' house. Elaine nonchalantly suggested that I call her Aunt Elaine. Although her request seemed to come out of nowhere, I was happy to do it since she was already like an aunt to me. She gave me loving hugs and always asked me to join them when she and my mother went shopping.

After I went to bed, Aunt Elaine decided to take up the issue about the possibility of me being her brother's child.

"Julie, are you sure Kalena ain't Larry's," she pressed.

"She's not! I told you that," my mother said.

My mother tried to change the subject, but Aunt Elaine was persistent with her quest to get to the truth. She was convinced that I was her niece because of my mother's vague answers and her body language. Aunt Elaine called her brother the next day to ask him to come to Ohio. She reminded him of the fling that he had with my mother years ago. She told him that she felt I was his daughter, deep down in my heart, I believe he know it already. My daddy was receptive to the idea of seeing me again and agreed to come to Cleveland. It took him nearly three months to work out the details to make the trip, but he finally showed up.

Aunt Elaine told my mother that she had spoken to her brother and that he was coming to see us. My mother started to feel anxious about the visit. And she contemplated revealing the truth to me. Years later she told me she needed to tell me. She couldn't bear the thought of this man coming to the house for a visit and not know he was my dad. She was still in love with my daddy despite the fact he betrayed her. She and Frank had recently divorced and was single. My mother thought she had a chance with him again. My daddy probably sweet-talked his way back into her life by telling her that he was coming to town to spend some time with her just to see me.

My daddy contacted my mother when he arrived and asked to see me. She desperately needed to clear her conscious, but the thought of coming clean had started to consume her; she was an emotional wreck. A few hours prior to his arrival I heard her sobbing profusely in the living room. I went to see what was wrong. For the second time, I connected with her on an emotional level and was able to really feel her pain. I cautiously walk over to her.

"What's wrong momma," I asked believing that she had gotten into another fight with Frank over my brothers or something.

"Tell me what's wrong?" I begged.

"I'm so sorry Kalena; I need to ask for forgiveness. I've lied to you all these years about your real dad."

"What about him, who is he?" I asked.

"His name is Larry Hullum, and he'll be coming over soon to see you," although my reaction to the news should've been an angry response it wasn't. I had been praying for a relationship with my daddy and God had answered my prayers. I hadn't been a Christian for that long, in fact, I was what some people would refer to me as a "Baby Christian," but I'd been down on my knees for years praying that the Lord would reveal to me who was my biological father. It was surreal! That morning I had gotten up early and was still prancing around the housed in my yellow bunny onesie. I gave my mother a loving hug and told her that she was forgiven.

"I love you Kalena, and always have I wanted you to have a relationship with your father, but I was selfish," she told me.

"I love you too mama don't worry I'm okay," I assured her before rushing off to my room to get dressed.

I wanted to look special for my first face to face meeting with my daddy. I picked out a pretty black dress and made sure that my hair and light make-up looked perfect. I was ready to show him how beautiful his daughter was who he missed out on years of her life although it wasn't his fault. I went back into the living room to wait on him. When he rang the doorbell, my mother went to answer it. I had butterflies in my stomach, and my palms were sweaty. When my daddy walked into the living room, I couldn't believe it, the man that was standing there looked just like I had imagined he would. He was tall, handsome, and seemed warm and inviting. I could see myself in him, and when he opened his mouth to say hello, I was mesmerized. All of my dreams had come true he was perfect to me. My mother introduced us right away, although there was some awkward silence in the room.

"Larry, we need to talk," my mother said. The instantly went out on the back porch to talk. Five minutes later, my mother calls me outside.

"Kalena, this is your father," she said.

"Hi daddy," I said nervously.

"I haven't seen you since you were two years old," he told me.

He caught me off guard when I heard him say that he hadn't seen me since I was two. I had believed all my life that he had left my mother hanging after she got pregnant and he didn't know I existed. At this point, it didn't matter I was happy to see him. We stayed on the back porch to make sure no one else could hear our conversation since we were living with Frank's family. I hung onto his every word, and I was happy to see my parents together on that porch it gave me a sense of comfort. We hit it off right away; he accepted me without question. It was reassuring since most black men don't go looking for more children to claim. My daddy told me that he wasn't married, and had other children. His first wife was a woman who my mother knew and was betrayed by. She had led him to California. It was apparent that my daddy liked stirring up trouble between my mother and women who she had been friends with.

My impression of him was that he could be a slick talking lady's man, but I didn't care about that or his checkered past. He had come to claim me, and it was the only thing that mattered. I wasn't going to allow him to walk out of my life by being judgmental. My daddy suggested that we go for a walk around the block so that we could get to know each other better. He told me all about his children and his family. He said that I had a lot of aunts, uncles, cousins, siblings, and grandparents who he wanted me to meet while he was there and apologized for not being in my life.

"I'm sorry that I wasn't there for you but I'm here now," he said. "I wasn't sure if you were my daughter, but I knew about you."

I listened quietly as he changed the topic to tell me about my half siblings. He said that I looked a lot like them and knew that we would hit it off. When walked back to my house after about thirty minutes he and my mother engaged in some small talk. He asked her if it was okay for me to meet his family while he was in town. She agreed that it was a great idea for me to get to know them finally. I was ecstatic! I thanked God for answering my prayers. I prayed for my mother too; I wanted God to forgive her for misleading me, most importantly allow her to forgive herself. I was old enough to understand that broken women do and say things that don't always serve them or their children well.

My daddy came back for me as promised. I got up early that next morning to pray prior to going with him to meet the family. I wanted to make a good impression on him, but it was apparent he wanted to do the same. He smelled great and looked polished even though he wore a casual jogging suit. He told me that our first stop would be at the hospital to visit his mother. He said that she had been sick and been in there for a few days. He wanted to make sure we had the opportunity to meet and said that she was always on his case about making certain that he claimed all his children because she had thought there was a possibility that she had another daughter.

We walked into my grandmother's room, she was alert and talking to some other family that had come to see her too. She immediately looked up when my daddy entered the room with me. I thought she was beautiful and as I observed her distinctive features. My daddy resembled her a lot, and I could tell that in her hay day she was one of those sophisticated church women who wore those Kentucky Derby hats regularly to church. She greeted me with a warm smile and seemed to be comfortable in my presence as though she already knew me. My daddy smiled like a Cheshire cat as he introduced us to each other.

"Mama, this is your granddaughter Kalena," he told her.

"Hello Kalena," she said as she gave me a quick once-over. "I'm so happy you came to see me," she said.

"Yes, ma'am, me too," I replied.

My daddy introduced me to the other's that were there. I decided to have a seat in the empty chair that was in the corner to observe my daddy and his family as they made a fuss over my grandmother. I was amazed by their language and family norms. They seemed close, something I was also use to with my mother's side of the family. I noticed that some of their mannerisms were similar to mine. I reached into my bag to pull out my bible. I wanted to read it while they talked about my grandmother's condition. I always had it with me. When my grandmother noticed me reading it, she struck up a conversation with me.

"I see you read the Bible child," she said.

"Yes ma 'mam, I've been studying it for a while," I replied confidently.

My grandmother was impressed that I had become a believer at such a young age. She told me that she was Pentecostal after I explained that I had become a Christian on July 17, 1988, and loved the Lord. It seemed our religion although different was something we had in common. She told me that she would be discharged soon and would love for me to visit her sometime. I agreed to visit since I wanted to get to know her better.

When we left the hospital, my daddy took me over to my grandmother's house. It was the place where a lot of families congregated all the time, and he had asked some of them to meet him there to meet me. My heart began beating faster as I anticipated meeting them. It was just like a scene right out of the Antwone Fisher movie. I couldn't believe how loving my father's family was towards me and I felt an immediate sense of belonging. I studied their faces and noticed everyone in the room looked like me in some way. Everyone started talking all at once as they tried to introduce themselves. I smiled and hugged each of them as I thought to myself how beautiful this experience was. I had to wait half my life to meet my daddy, and it was worth it.

My daddy dropped me off later that night and made plans to visit me every day while he was there and when it came time for him to leave, we exchanged information so that we could stay in contact. He said that I could come to visit him anytime. My faith in God grew stronger because of my encounter with my daddy. I started visiting his mother regularly, and every time I went to her house, she introduced me to more family. I gleamed with pride every time I met a new family member.

My grandmother would say, "This is Larry's child," with pride.

I remember the first time I met my daddy's brother, Eddie. I thought now here's someone whose demeanor matches mine. He was different than the others, and it showed every time you spoke to him. He was feisty, and his words could cut if he were aggravated. I didn't like him at first because I thought he was mean. He didn't seem to like children or young adults. I wanted to be adored by him and all the Hullum clan.

Uncle Eddie was old school. He'd tell you off at a moment's notice. After some reflection, I realized that I was just like him. It was an "Ah Ha" moment for me, and after that, he started to grow on me the more I was around him. My words were cutting too, and I could use them to hurt people just like Uncle Eddie. I realized that I had inherited this trait and didn't have to feel like I was the only person in the world that was like that. I also noticed that the Hullum men, in my daddy's family, were aggressive in nature, but Uncle Eddie was definitely the most colorful out of the bunch.

My daddy called me a few times a month and then continued to strengthen our relationship. When my Aunt Elaine came back over to hang out with my mother, she said that she was happy that I was her "real" niece and she teased my mother about her deception every time she came over. I finally felt completed I had both sides of my family and even Frank's to love me and I felt special.

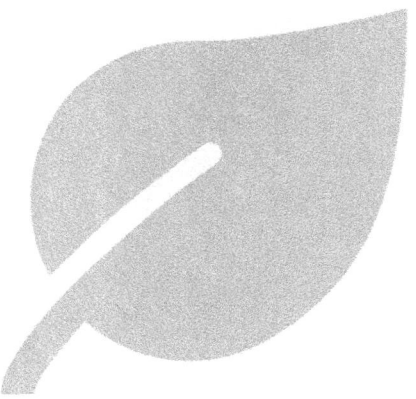

CHAPTER 7

Reflection

I thought my Aunt Elaine was a very nice fun lady but didn't realize that she was family back then. She had always been around in my physical space, and her visual image never left me. I loved to play with her children who were my cousins. Kids are flexible and will play with anyone. As a child, I wasn't able to comprehend the dynamics between Aunt Elaine and my mother. She was always in my mother's life, and they seem to enjoy each other's company. At some point, I stopped playing with her kids and didn't see her family anymore. To this day I don't know why. Aunt Elaine was a fashionista who reminded me of Patti Labelle with her mannerism. She was and still is my favorite Aunt. I felt very complete and whole like I was in a fairy tale when I saw daddy for the first time. I was able to connect to him instantly. I thought he was modern, tall, and had a kind demeanor. My daddy had a commanding presence and stood 6'4 with an athletic built. I noticed right away that I had his eyes. I had often wondered where I got my eyes from. I learned the power of "asking" in faith and believing that I would get it. That's what brought my daddy to me. It was magical and better than I could imagine. I was nervous and emotional! I recall breaking down in his arms when he hugged me for the first time. He was the miracle that I prayed for, and God gave me more than I had asked for. It was great to have a praying spiritually grandmother that was the same color as me. My grandmother had a loving and welcoming spirit. I loved the way she allowed me to share my faith with her. I felt like God sent me her to share my power with her and she eventually helped me with my purpose and to find what I was called to do in Christ. The Hullum's were loving I learned that I was grandchild number 45. There were a lot of moving parts and people to get to know. Nick and Sally Hullum, my grandparents, had nine children and I gained a large family. My Uncle Eddie reminded me that I was part of the Hullum bloodline. He had a rough life and seemed to mean whether he was playing or not. My mother said that I reminded her of him because he could speak his mind but not always in a way that made others feel warm and fuzzy just like me. I remained poised and polite when I was around my daddy's family until I could learn my footing.

CHAPTER 8

Power of Being His

A month prior to my eighteenth birthday, I received the greatest gift of all. Jesus Christ became my Lord and personal savior. I was hungry for a relationship with him since no one up to that point had told me that it was okay for a child to seek one. I was waiting for that special moment when God would tap me on the shoulder and say in His ever so sweet voice that it was possible. However, it didn't happen like that. God sent a good friend to stir up my desire for a personal relationship with Him, and where I would eventually ask for one.

Nick was a childhood friend who lived in our neighborhood when we were little. He was like a brother to me, and he and Dwight were best friends. We had gone to elementary school together. When we finished Junior High, we noticed that Nick's demeanor had changed. He was hanging out with the wrong crowd, becoming a little rough around the edges, and what some people would describe as a thug. He was known for his ability to rap lyrics, something a lot of guys were into at the time. They thought the keys to their success was to become a rapper. Luckily for him, his family moved away from the area before he got into some serious trouble. Dwight lost contact with him after his family moved.

I thought about Nick often and wondered what happened to him. I thought perhaps he had gotten locked up or worst was dead. About a year later, we happened to run into him. He had moved with his family around the corner from us. He and Dwight were able to rekindle their friendship. On the surface, he seemed like the same person who had left years ago, but to our surprise, we quickly learned that he was an entirely different person. He hung out with positive people and showed the potential for leadership. The thing that I liked about the "new" Nick was that he was on fire for the Lord. I found myself wanting to hang around him to hear how his transformation happened and if there was a way for me to have the same experience.

Nick was ready to make his mark in the world. We started hanging out at a familiar friend's house who lived down the street from him. Nick would share the word of God with our close circle of friends and me. I loved the way he witnessed; his eloquent interpretation of the word fed my spirit. His testimony caused me to examine my life and to deepen my relationship with God. Growing up, I went to church occasionally with family members and had been briefly introduced to religion. Up until that point, my opinions about the goodness of God were based on someone else's experience, and I wanted to know Him for myself.

Dwight and Nick's relationship seem to falter. Dwight wasn't interested in learning or hearing the word, but I'd show up every day to hear him testify. Our close group of friends who listened to him witness got smaller each day, and it wasn't too long before it was just the two of us sitting on the porch in the evenings to talk about the goodness of the Lord. Our friends were tired of focusing on the Bible for hours; however, I'd listen attentively to what Nick had to share no matter how long or late it got. He taught me so much, and I was impressed with his ability to repeat scriptures and meditating on their meaning.

I was now a senior in my last year of high school, and the need for me to be on patrol at home was no longer necessary. After school on most evenings, I'd go over to Nick's house to talk. He can be credited for helping me find my way out of the darkness after my decision to abort my child. It was easy for me to open up about my life and experiences with my ex-boyfriend Shank. I was still feeling stressed and hopeless, and our breakup forced me to look at life differently. I had built up a wall of defense and was reluctant to share how I was feeling, but the pain was tearing me apart. I regretted the fact that my ex and I had wasted so many years, and that it took us so long to recognize the fact that we wanted different things out of life.

Nick's presence gave me hope. He helped me reconnect with the parts of me that were lost. After spending about a month together, Nick asked me to attend bible study with him. His persistence finally paid off; eventually, I agreed to go. He attended Bible Study at the Hasberrys' house, a popular couple who lived in our neighborhood. Jerri White taught the class every Wednesday night. I was hooked after the first time I went and wanted to continue to be with other believers. A small group of us would gather around their living room to have fellowship and to praise God.

I felt safe and in good company with them. They prayed for one another and for me the first time I went, apparently, they knew I needed it. I felt an awakening that night. It was a feeling that I couldn't explain, but looking back it felt as if I had received a deep surge of power that seemed to have taken over my body. I desired to be in that room, at that moment, with those believers.

I went to Bible Study a few more times with Nick, and the more I went, the more I experienced a breakthrough. He asked me to go to church with him believing that it was time for me to take the next step since I enjoyed Bible Study so much. I came up with an excuse not to go. I told him that I wasn't ready to make a commitment. It was hard to tell Nick no, but I knew if I said yes, he would expect me to go all the time.

"Kalena, you should come to church with me," he said.

"I don't have anything to wear," I told him.

"I'm not going to let the fact that you don't have anything to wear stop you from growing in the Lord. I'll buy you some clothes." He told me.

I wasn't sure if Nick was serious, but he asked me for my sizes and went to the mall without me. He showed up later with a large bag and handed it to me. I looked inside and found a nice pantsuit. I loved it! I couldn't believe that he had such good taste. He took away my excuse not to go. His willingness to encourage me to have a personal relationship with God made me feel closer to him. I made a commitment to take my relationship to the next level. Nick bragged to everyone in our Bible Study class that I was going to church with him. They encouraged and supported my decision to go too.

When we arrived at church that following Sunday, I felt at home as soon as we walked in. I marveled at the beauty of the sanctuary and was welcomed right away by the congregation. The name of the church was Light of Liberty, and the minister was Pastor Melvin Warren. We sat down in the pew near the front of the church. I noticed how intentional everyone seems to be as they listened to the preacher who stood in the pulpit. He instructed them to open their Bibles to John 3:16. I took my personal Bible out of my purse and turned there too. I finally landed on John 3:16 after a few minutes. Up until that point, I didn't know where all the books in the Bible were located even though I read it often. I had learned a lot of scriptures and had even memorized some just like Nick. I continued to attend Bible Study and to find out more about the word. Eventually, I felt comfortable enough to share my thoughts with our group. I began attending church often and could feel the spirit of God moving in the church. I had become a true believer.

Nick and I were developing deeper feelings for each other. He was everything that I imagined a boyfriend should be. Nick was strong, charismatic, and dependable. We began dating seriously, and it didn't take him long to ask me to marry him. He asked right in front of our congregation. Nick and our pastor conspired to make his proposal special. Of course, I said YES! We decided not to rush things and planned a long engagement. We were inseparable and assumed leadership roles in the youth ministry. The youth gravitated to us. They loved our trailblazing teaching and public affection for God. We talked about taking our ministry to the next level.

We had planned to go to college together. We applied and were accepted to Moody's Bible Institute in Chicago. It seemed like God was ordering our footsteps. When we received our acceptance letters to Moody our church celebrated the news with us. We couldn't wait to move away from Cleveland to pursue our dreams. I was so happy but I had started to question the stability of our relationship. Before running off to Chicago I wanted to make sure we shared the same level of commitment to one another. It was a major decision, and I had to consider the cost to attend. I didn't want to add any additional financial burdens for my family. I decided to remain in Cleveland, but I worried if I was making the right decision.

Nick stayed in Cleveland for the summer and we continued seeing each other. Our inner circle of friends never allowed our being young Christians to deter us from doing things young adults did like hanging out, watching movies, or going out to eat. We spent a lot of our leisure time with friends at each other's houses. However, Nick and I decided to cool our heels and only hang out together on the weekends. We wanted to spend more time with our families. Our decision changed things between us even though we were engaged. It never dawned on me that it would eventually cause our breakup. I ignored the red flags when I noticed Darleece's car parked down the street at the Hasberry's house. I noticed that Nick was over there to which wasn't too unusual since we all rode in each other's cars too. I asked Nick what was going on. I failed to dig deeper to find out why he wasn't at his house spending time with his family like we agreed. Darleece and Nick began having a fling behind my back. It was a slap in the face since she and I were really good friends.

I was angry with myself for being so naïve. My gut was screaming something is wrong, but I failed to trust it. I found out that Nick wasn't the standup guy that I thought he was. We were supposed to be in a serious relationship and to be married.

Nick followed his dreams, and in the fall, he left for Chicago to attend Moody's Bible College. Darleece and I were left in Cleveland to figure things out the hard way. I would run into her at church, and I will never forget the day I learned that Nick asked her to marry him too. There was a group of our mutual friends surrounding Darleece, and she had their undivided attention. I walked over to them to see what all the laughter was about. I could tell that they were talking about something special.

"What's going on over here," I asked.

"I'm getting married to Nick," Darleece bragged.

My heart sank, I couldn't believe what I was hearing. I felt humiliated, she told them that they set the date and would get married in July. I was furious with Nick for leading me on, and for allowing me to wear his ring in the church where he had proposed to me. I wanted to run and hide. My power was depleted and a sense of emptiness set in. I knew something was off since Nick didn't call me while he was in Chicago, and when we talked our conversations lacked the warmth they used to have.

I couldn't believe that he had betrayed me. I was furious and officially broke things off with him. I tried to keep my head up, but it was difficult since I didn't stop going to Bible Study and our church. The word circulated around the church quickly. Everyone asked questions about what happened. I decided to move in with the Hasberry's who had become my Godparents. I wanted to continue my involvement in church. They gave me a rental contract which I paid fifty dollars a month in cash and seventy-five dollars in Food Stamps. I was able to receive them since I was a college student living on my own. My mom moved across town to be closer to my grandparents. She gave me her blessing, and I appreciated her doing so, because it would have been hard for me to make it from way across town to get to church and Bible Study. I wasn't going to allow anyone or anything to interfere with my relationship with God.

Nick and I had let the youth down and our pastor too. He demanded we address the mess we created, and he recommended that we participate in counseling sessions with him before Nick married Darleece. I knew I needed some closure, but the pain I felt immobilized me, and I was stuck.

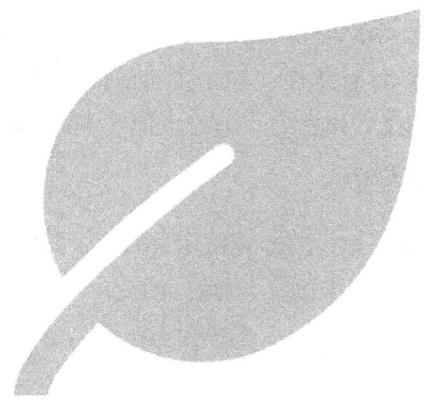

CHAPTER 8

Reflection

I realized that my relationship with Shank was based on my infatuation with him. I had come to grips with the fact that what I felt for him was not love but my feelings were very intense. I attached a soul tie to him because he was the first of a lot of things for me. My actions in his presence were confusing, and I fell victim to him. There was no substance to our relationship. Shank slow walked me and groomed me for sex as most teenaged boys do. I had a sexual relationship with him and was connected in that way. My thinking was faulty at times which led to inappropriate behaviors. I didn't have my daddy or any other male role models to affirm my beauty or to build up my self-esteem. Shank was able to communicate what I yearned to hear from a popular young man who others wanted for themselves. He didn't have my best interest at hand. When Nick rejected me, it was different. I was distraught beyond measure, and we didn't have a sexual relationship. We enjoyed a relationship full of substances and depth. We chose to honor our covenant and commitment to God. We had our thinking caps on and were making the right decisions. Nick's betrayal was the lowest thing that anyone could've done to me. I loved him. We had history and friendship; I didn't know how to handle his betrayal. His rejection was the ultimate rejection that any woman could experience, and I was no different. My heart ached for years. I thank God that my negative experience with Nick didn't allow me to hate men for the rest of my life.

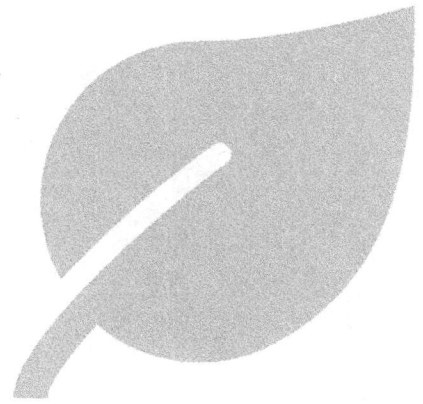

CHAPTER 9

Power of Being Mrs. James

God knew exactly what he was doing when he sent Vaughn James to me; however, I wasn't ready to receive him. In fact, the first time I met Vaughn I thought he was an arrogant jerk. I was in recovery from my heartbreak with Nick and wanted some space. I was still in a dark place, and if the truth were told, I couldn't find my way out of the darkness. The thought of being hurt by another man and allow him to take my power wasn't something that I was going to let happen again. Which is why Vaughn's confident demeanor rubbed me the wrong way.

I decided to pursue my education by enrolling in Tri-C College in Cleveland. I was still feeling the ramifications from my decision to not go to Moody's Bible College. Pursuing my education was also going to give me a way to get over Nick. It felt good to have a distraction and to be in a different head space. I had to ride the bus to get downtown to where Tri-C was located. After I finished the first semester, I felt strong enough to take some more classes. So I pushed on to the second semester, and enrolled in a Computer Processing class that was held on Saturday mornings. It was a combination class consisting of a lecture and a lab.

I recall the first day of class. I couldn't wait to get the day started, because computers were the new craze and I wanted to be part of it. I ran most of the way to the bus stop that morning. The air was brisk, so I wore my favorite leather bomber coat to keep me warm. I got downtown about a half an hour before the start time. I looked for the classroom and after I found it, I sat on the floor in the hallway and waited. I was looking at the syllabus when a young man wearing a red Ohio State jacket, and ripped stonewashed jeans approached me. He had a motorcycle helmet in his hand, so I assumed he rode his bike to class. He didn't hesitate to try to get my attention by making what I perceived to be a rude comment.

"It's a little too hot to be wearing that jacket don't you think?" He said.

"I catch colds easily," I replied.

He was handsome and physically fit, but I was turned off by his attitude. I thought he was a punk. I said to myself, "Who does this punk think he is; besides it's none of his business what I'm wearing." I wanted him to leave me alone, but he didn't. He continued his line of questioning and asked what kind of music and movies I liked. I had two problems with him, the first was I didn't want his attention, and the second was that I was still in love with Nick.

I answered his questions before walking into the classroom. I quickly sat in one of the empty seats closest to the window. I tried to make eye contact with some of the other students as they walked into the class. I was trying to get them to take up the other seats around me. I didn't want the arrogant young man to sit by me. Luckily, he was forced to sit on the other side of the classroom. When the class started the professor asked us to introduce ourselves. He pointed at me to go first. I knew that the young man would be listening intently to learn my name. I confidently introduced myself to the class.

"My name is Kalena Fitzgerald," I blurted out.

Several other students went after me, and when it was his turn my ears perked up.

"Vaughn James," he said then sat in the seat.

I thought he's even arrogant when asked to introduce himself. He was equipped with my name, and I knew he'd use it. When the class was over I made a beeline to the door, to avoid Vaughn. I wanted to get as far away from him as I could. I accomplished my goal, which was to make sure he didn't follow me. When I got home I immediately sank back into a state of depression. It seemed no matter how hard I tried, I couldn't seem to shake it off. My feelings of betrayal were hard to ignore. My world seemed to be spinning out of control. I tried my best to remain focused on my education despite my dissatisfaction with my life. Living with the Hasberry's didn't help much, they supported Nick and Darleece and were going to be in their wedding. Their daughter Latrice and I had become best friends. She was the only one who seemed to be supportive of me. She'd challenged me when I was wrong, and listened when I need a shoulder to cry on. I could push through my pain whenever we talked.

The following Saturday I caught the bus to class as usual. On the way there I started thinking about Vaughn. I knew I'd have to deal with him and decided to act like I didn't see him, but when I arrived he wasn't there yet. I waited outside again for class to start, and I noticed Vaughn out of the corner of my eye walking down the hallway. He was dressed up in a suit, and had on a long leather trench coat with a briefcase in hand. I thought he was completely overdressed, and I couldn't resist the chance to get even with him by commenting on his clothing.

"Do you always come to class dressed like that? I said.

"I've got an interview after class," he told me.

I felt a little silly after hearing his answer. I was impressed by the fact that he was different from other guys I knew. Vaughn was a lot more mature. When class started our instructor directed us into the lab. I tried to get a seat away from him but he was clever. He jumped in the empty seat next to me before anyone else could. I knew he was interested in me, but I didn't feel the same way about him. He asked me the same questions about my movies, and music preference again. "You can't be rude girl," I told myself. So I forced myself to answer his questions. The instructor gave us the list of materials needed for the class, and suggested we purchase them before class met again. I took a look at the list and prayed that I had enough money to cover the cost. After class I walked to the bookstore with a friend. Vaughn walked closely behind us. He watched me as I placed the items on the list in my plastic basket. I was looking for a floppy disk when I heard Vaughn's voice.

"Did you find what you were looking for?" he asked.

"Yes, but I'll be two dollars short I think," I told him although I was embarrassed.

"I'll pay the two dollars," he told me.

I would have to put something back and get it the following week if I refused to let Vaughn help me. I told myself again "don't be rude girl," I thanked him for his kindness.

I thought about an exit, I wanted to get away from him. I didn't want him to get too comfortable, and believe he had a reason now to talk to me because he paid the two dollars. I excused myself and walked quickly toward the elevator and stepped inside. When the door opened there were two older women inside waiting to go down. I walked in and pushed the button for the first floor, but before the door closed Vaughn slipped inside.

"Oh no," I thought. I tried not to make eye contact with him; however, he didn't care that the two ladies were listening. He started talking right away. I played along so that I didn't seem rude, but I prayed he wouldn't ask me out. It took the elevator forever to get to the first floor giving Vaughn time to find out more about me. By the time the elevator door opened he had asked me out on a date. I felt trapped, and those noisy women were hanging on our every word.

"Kalena can I take you to dinner and a movie sometime," he asked.

"YES," I told him while trying not to let on that I was annoyed.

Vaughn pulled out a piece of paper and asked me to write my telephone number and address on it. I wrote down my contact information and excused myself. He told me that he would pick me up around eight. As I walked to the bus stop my mind was racing. I didn't want to go out on a date with Vaughn. I planned to come up with an excuse not to go, but he didn't call when I expected him to.

I was relieved! I took a nap but was awaken by the phone ringing. It was my best friend Lelisa on the other end. She was distraught and crying hysterically. She had just broken up with her boyfriend and needed some support. I wanted to comfort her and let her know I knew exactly how she felt. I told her that I would come over. So I quickly changed my clothes. When I opened the door to leave, Vaughn was standing on my doorstep. I couldn't believe he had the nerve to come over without calling first. Even though he said our date would be at eight.

I decided to go with the flow since I needed to take my mind off of my problems. I thought Vaughn would be a good distraction. I told him that I couldn't stay out long because my best friend was having a crisis and needed me. He didn't seem to mind that our dinner at Mountain Jacks be interrupted. I was impressed by his ability to take me to dinner at a fancy restaurant that would cost over a hundred dollars.

During dinner I saw Vaughn in a new light. He was a natural conversationalist with a broad worldview. I was drawn to his intelligence and outlook on life in general. My life paled in comparison, it was evident that he had a good childhood and was spoiled. We were in our early twenties and he already owned a fancy muscle car and a Kawasaki motorcycle. Those were material things that a girl my age would gravitate to. I liked the fact that I didn't have to worry about running into anyone I knew, because we didn't run in the same circles.

After we finished our dinner I asked Vaughn to take me to Lelisa's house so I could provide a shoulder to cry on. I felt like I needed a good cry too. When we got there I invited Vaughn to come inside to meet her. Some of my other friends had also came over. I wanted him to know that I was a person of integrity and wasn't just blowing him off. He came in briefly to meet them and left shortly after introductions were made. I continued to spend time with Vaughn, but I purposely kept him at bay from my friends and church family. I didn't want him to know that I was still in love with Nick, and if given the opportunity they would tell him all of my secrets.

I began to notice that whenever I was with Vaughn the dark cloud that hung over my head was lifted, and he made me laugh. However, I wasn't ready to jump into a serious relationship. As Nick and Darleece's wedding day got closer I thought a serious relationship wouldn't be a bad idea. It actually started to look promising. They planned to get married in July, but little did I know Nick was feeling guilty about betraying me. A week before his wedding he came over to see me. I was on the phone talking to Vaughn, so I asked if I could call him back. I was surprised to see him standing on my porch. Seeing Nick didn't help anything. All of my feelings for him came boiling to the surface, but I tried to act nonchalant. He looked sad, and he looked like he had a lot on his mind.

"I wanted to check on you, and to make sure that you're okay," he said.

"I'm doing okay," I lied.

Nick told me that he wouldn't go through with his wedding if it were going to cause me to fall away from God. I was taken aback and couldn't believe that he had the nerve to try to make me feel that I had the power to choose for him. We had been best friends, confidants, and a team who vowed to change the world together. I told him that I forgave him and that he was free to move on, but I made him promise that he would never forget our friendship. He gave me a loving hug and said that he wouldn't. When he walked away, I felt abandoned and helpless. He was moving on with his life, and it didn't include me. Darleece was getting what I was promised, and I was angry.

I couldn't escape hearing the details of their wedding. My Godparents were always talking about it and what was happening. Every time I heard them talking reminded me that I was dumped. The congregation even gossiped behind my back about my failed relationship with Nick, and not to mention the way they looked at me when they talked about it. The pity in their eyes made me self-conscious and ashamed. I felt like a wounded duck.

I believe God sends our mates and it's up to us to discern who that person is, because they may not look like the person we envisioned. I must admit, I wanted to be with Vaughn for selfish reasons. I'd asked myself "Kalena who are you kidding, you're not ready for this sweet man?" Vaughn was exceptional and deserved someone who would give him their heart completely. Sadly, that person wasn't me.

Nick hurt me deeply. I lost a lot of weight and had to be hospitalized for a few days, and I was down to about 100lbs. My doctor said my Asthma was inflamed and that it was causing my chest muscles to collapse. It was hard to eat and sleep, and I seriously contemplated suicide. I thought it would be the best way to get away. I didn't tell Vaughn what I was going through, and he didn't notice I had lost weight. I decided to get even with Nick, and my uncertain future-self by committing to a rebound relationship with Vaughn.

I actually wanted to attend Nick and Darleece's ceremony, but I decided to go to another friend's wedding instead. I received several different accounts of how things went. One of which was, as the pastor wrapped up their wedding by charging the guest "to speak now or forever hold your piece," he purposely remained silent for over two minutes. The pastor was conflicted and wanted to rejoice and cry at the same time, because he knew someone was happy and someone was sad. He was a pastor to all of us. He wanted to end all of the drama that had gone on for the last few months. He was trying to do that by challenging anyone who opposed to the union to say so, but no one said a word.

Things escalated quickly between Vaughn and me. We were starting to hint to each other that we should get married.

"How long does it take to plan a wedding?" I asked him attempting to test the waters.

"A couple of months," he replied. "You just need a tux, dress, and a pastor," he added not knowing that I was serious.

I wanted to redeem my life that was taken away from me. My suggestion earned me a marriage proposal of sorts. We planned to marry in August even though I was conflicted. I was conflicted because I was a Christian familiar with the principals of marriage. It caused me to consider if my actions were appropriate, but I believed that getting married to Vaughn was something that needed to happen right away. After all, Nick had gotten married and I wasn't going to be left out.

My family pitched in and planned a five-hundred-dollar wedding for Vaughn and me. Even though I was getting what I wanted, I wasn't happy. The night of my Bachelorette party I questioned my actions, but I'd had come too far to call things off. I remember walking outside to clear my thoughts. My grandmother followed me, because she wanted to know what was wrong. She knew me better than anyone, but I pretended like everything was okay. Only family and some close friends were invited since a lot of my friends had been loyal to Nick. My god sister Latrice told me she wouldn't participate in this mess. She knew I still loved Nick. It was supposed to be a happy day, but it wasn't because my church family wasn't included. As I stood at the altar I had a conversation with

God. I asked him to come down and stop me, because I knew I was out of order. I stood there with an offended heart feeling abandoned by my church and questioning God's plan. I felt rejected by the love of my life, but I went through with my wedding to Vaughn anyway. He believed he hit the lottery by marrying me, but if the truth be told I was the lucky one. He had to deal with me until I obtained the spiritual maturity needed to sustain a healthy marriage with him.

I asked my pastor to provide me counseling behind Vaughn's back. I was really struggling with bitterness towards Darleece and the facade of being happy in a marriage. I had the opportunity to forgive Nick, but not her. I was angry with her and needed to forgive her and myself. After a few months passed I felt compelled to let Vaughn know how I felt. Pastor Warren told me I owed my husband the opportunity to decide if he wanted to remain married to me or not, because I married him out of false pretenses.

"Vaughn, I don't want you to be mad at me, I've been meeting with Pastor Warren about Nick. Remember when I told you I was over him?" "Well, I wasn't, I married you out of a rebound. I don't love you like you love me, but I'm willing to try." I confessed. I continued to tell him, "Pastor said that you have the right to leave me, but it was important for me to be honest because I need your forgiveness and I want to make this marriage work." I said.

Vaughn was devastated. The blow I delivered nearly destroyed him. I had never seen him cry, and as I watched him my heart broke for him too.

"I married you out of an offense, but I want to love you," I told him.

Vaughn was too distraught to process what my confession meant for us. In the days that followed Vaughn wore his heartbreak on his sleeve, but he wanted to save our marriage. Vaughn loved me, and he was intentional about making things work. I wanted to work things out too, and because God sent Vaughn to me he helped turn things around. I learned a powerful lesson during that time. I found out that the people we care about deserve to be treated with respect, and if you're not transparent with them the consequence is a depletion of your personal power.

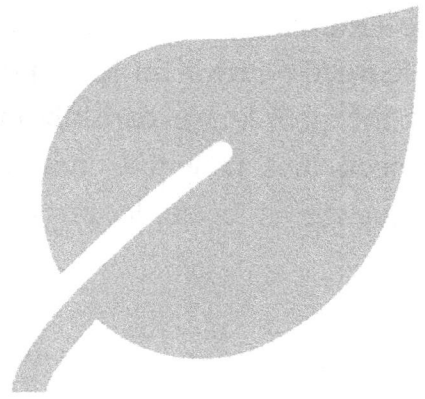

CHAPTER 9

Reflection

As an African American woman, I was taught to be strong and not allow others to take advantage of me. It's a cultural thing that weighed heavily on my heart. It was hard to get past the exterior walls I built because of the fear I felt. A lot of black women have a mantra that usually goes along these lines "You bet not let no man treat you any kind of way," or "Don't let no man run over you." These were the things my mother told me also, her voice echoed her sentiment in my ears during those early years as I explored relationships with the opposite sex. She said what she believed those boys wanted from me, and even gave me advice on how to halt their efforts. She set the standard for what love should look like, how we should protect ourselves from those who wish to abuse it.

God began to work on my heart, and I gave Him the opportunity to lead me. He helped me overcome the offense of what happened to me in my relationship with Nick. I kept my heart in reserve for a long time and refused to surrender to anyone. I was afraid, vulnerable, and didn't want to yield to love. God continue to ask me to allow him to work on my behalf. I was slowly able to surrender, although the process hurt since I believed that my trust and love would be eventually violated. I was falling in love with Vaughn, and he was the first person who I allowed past my internal barriers, but I kept my guard up. I was afraid that he would hurt me. I began to speculate and became accusatory towards him blaming my paranoid thoughts on him. Thank God for grace. I was anxious, nervous, and could no longer rely on my psyche that was pushing back against the bullies I faced, my mother, my step-father, the predators who prey on me, and everything else that cause me trauma throughout my life. I realized that Vaughn was a good man who could love, protect, and be faithful to me which were all the things I built a wall to reject. God pushed me beyond those walls, and I surrender my love to Vaughn. My internal barriers came to the forefront, and I was able to release and experience a deeper love for him. I found myself trusting him with "ME." No longer was I the fragile, wounded woman, he made me feel whole, protected and loved. I enjoyed what Vaughn's love meant, and it felt right to receive it.

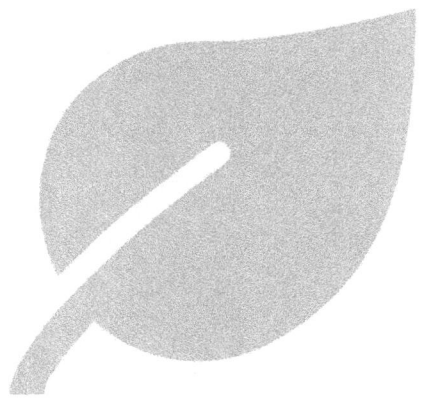

CHAPTER 10

Purpose Finding Way

God had always shown me a glimpse of my purpose. Even back in those days when I was treated poorly by my mother and Frank, disrespected by Shank, humiliated by Nick, and loved by Vaughn. Slowly but surely I banked those teaching moments and powerful lessons knowing that I'd eventually be on sure footing. I was ready to connect and walk in my purpose. I had a new life, and it looked different from the one I had dreamed about at that juncture. Life at first glance seemed like a setback. I was a Christian who had accepted the Lord a few months before my eighteenth birthday, so I had assumed that finding my purpose was something that would come easy. At the pinnacle of my life I believed I was operating in my true purpose when Nick and I were together. We were going to conquer the world, by now you all know how that turned out!

I married Vaugh James at twenty-one, had my first child at twenty-two, my second at twenty-three, and in 1994 at the age of twenty-four relocated to Kokomo. The first part of my twenties was spent building a family and nurturing my relationships with my husband and children. We'd come a long way. Midway through I began to reexamine my life by exploring my purpose through my relationship with my Lord and Savior. Which had always been my place of reconciliation, since I loved to spend time talking to God. I realized that my twenties were a pivotal part and crucial time for self-development and direction. As a young wife and mother, I often felt like I placed my life on a shelf to meet the obligations of my family. My heart began yearning for additional servitude, and my inner spirit I knew I had more to give to others besides my family. That was my purpose!

Vaughn and I plugged into a local church in 1996, and we didn't waste any time asking to serve. I was introduced to Sister Sherri Mills, the church's Music Minister and Fine Arts Coordinator. After she interviewed me and learned how I could help out, I was given the position of church decorator. I was responsible for coordinating the logistics of decorating for the nearly thousand-person congregation. I was delighted to be of service to them. You name it, I did! I created the ambiance for each occasion, Christmas, Thanksgiving, Pastor Appreciation, Tithers banquet or whatever our Pastor called the event. I learned through decorating that I could serve others by creating an experience for them on both an individual and collective level. I served in this capacity for three years.

I continued to find ways to operate in my purpose. As I look back on other life changing moments that God used to show me my purpose, I recall some peaks of purpose worth mentioning. The Friendship Home was one such opportunity. The home closed in 2008. It was my first and foremost opportunity to support and minister to young people who were dear to my heart. It was a group home for girls living away from their families. It was my first leadership role given to me under our church with the Women to Women ministry leader at FWC. I was able to explore my gift of creating content and information. This content and information would help someone's internality shift to accept personal responsibility for personal opportunities to live better lives. These young group of girls were away from home and had limited financial resources.

The National Prayer Day held in 1989 in public square, was significant to me I wanted to share prayer with people from all faiths to pray for our nation. Doing so would also help to infuse my purpose in a universal way. I was always praying for young people my age, but I was ready to widen my net. My best friend Lelisa and I felt like we were destined to be there. The event was going to be at the IX

Center, which was out near the airport. We would have to rely on rapid transit to get us to the airport, and after that it was anyone's guess how we would get there. We only had two dollars, and it was going to cost a lot more money than that to get there.

We had a plan, we'd use one dollar to go and another to get back. We managed to make it to the airport, but once we got there we found out that the IX Center wasn't as close to the airport than we believed. We were wandering around the parking lot area when an airport worker gave us directions. He explained that we would have to walk up a ramp and cross the freeway to get there. We were perplexed yet determined to get there. At first, when Lelisa and I heard the word "adjacent" we assumed that meant right next door to the airport. He also explained that we could ride the airport shuttle to get to the end of the ramp before walking up. It was dark out, and we had come to a dead end. We were standing in front of a steep ramp. Things looked bleak and nearly impossible, but we weren't going to miss the event.

Lelisa and I looked at each other and said hell or high water, and against all the odds we weren't going to quit. Our desire to make it to the National Day of Prayer was burning in our hearts that day. An airport employee pulled up in a truck, asked us where we were going. He offered to carry us up the ramp, and although we had no knowledge of his character, we threw caution to the wind and hopped inside his truck. You'd think I'd be a little more cautious after my previous experiences with stranger danger in the past, but we figured it was two against one and God had our back.

Before we could get settled in the back of the truck, a car pulled up with a woman and her teenaged daughter inside. She asked for directions to the IX Center and said that she had gotten lost and wanted to get there on time. The man rattled off the directions, but stopped in midsentence to tell her that he had two female passengers inside that were going there too. He asked her to give us a ride there. Lelisa and I were in disbelief, and couldn't believe an angel was standing in front of us.

We hopped in the woman's vehicle, and it only took her a few minutes to get there. We witnessed to the woman and her daughter our perseverance, and the challenges we had gone through. We offered her the two dollars we had left to our name for gas after she offered to take us home after the event was over. We dispersed into the crowd when we got there and hooked up with several of our friends. They listened to us as we repeated the day's trials and tribulations. We knew we were in the right place, the Prayer Meeting was everything we thought it would be. We met the woman at her car when it was over and shared our individual testimonies of when we first accepted Christ. The woman couldn't believe how young we were. God worked with us to share our faith. We never asked the woman anything about her or her daughter. We just wanted to share our faith and the gospel.

Two weeks later the women showed up at our church with a praise report. She recalled our conversation about where we went to church. She told us that we had a profound effect on her and her daughter. She said that her daughter had accepted the Lord the week before at their home church. Lelisa and I were so excited about what God had done in the lives of others.

It was compelling to have a voice and be able to use it to convey my power. I realized that people's lives mattered and there are common threads that connect us. Stories matter, and how we overcome great odds do too. Linking to other people's threads is powerful.

Another powerful moment for me was on a Greyhound Bus I took from Cleveland to Indianapolis. I was headed to Kokomo to see my daddy who had sent for me to spend the summer with him. He kept his promise to have a relationship with me. It was my first-time riding on the bus, and I was excited and nervous at the same time. I sat in the very front seat on the right-hand side, so I could see out of the window, get on and off the bus safely, and relax.

I recall the bus driver making a stop somewhere in Columbus Ohio when a young college student got on. She surveyed the bus to see where she wanted to sit. Thankfully, the Lord directed her to sit in the empty seat next to me, but little did I know I would end up sharing my faith with the young woman. I struck up a conversation with her right away. She gravitated to me and seemed to feel comfortable. I recall talking the entire time. She told me that she was on her way home to visit her parents. Her visit was intentional, she had been diagnosed with Cervical Cancer and needed the courage to share the news with her parents.

Her questions to me were strategic. She wanted to know about God, death, forgiveness, and the afterlife. I thanked God for equipping me with the ability to sit there and mode into her world. I was able to provide her with a sense of peace and hope. I was able to use my voice to be the best witness and example of a Christian I could be. My purpose was clear, to connect with people in their darkest hour or to cheerlead them in their greatest outcome. I dared them to dream, and grow. I helped others by bringing wisdom and clarity by sharing wisdom and truth with them, and inspiring them to take action no matter the outcome.

One Christmas, the faith I had in God helped me to teach the lesson of purpose to my daughter. We joined another mother-daughter team to bless a couple of families for the Christmas holiday. We went out into the community, and while in the car decided to pray about which house we'd bless. When we went to the first house we dropped off the groceries, and as we walked away from the front door the family returned home. We didn't stay long; we only said Merry Christmas and told them we just wanted to be a blessing.

We drove around to the next house praying for single women in the area. We wanted to advocate for women in need during the holidays. We took our daughters to help demonstrate the teachings of random acts of kindness and its effect. The lesson was that it didn't take a lot to present a bag of groceries to a woman who perhaps didn't have the money to purchase the items themselves for Christmas. Things like potatoes, canned green beans, a turkey, and dessert. We went to a familiar neighborhood and knocked on the next door. A woman answered that we recognized. She went to our church and had a daughter with some medical problems. We had no idea that it was her house, but we knew that God had sent us there in that moment of need. My daughter still practices random acts of kindness today.

Being part of the outreach ministry at church gave me plenty of opportunities to explore my purpose. I teamed up with a few volunteers, and we'd go to Kinsey Youth Center once a week for an hour. We worked with the troubled young women who seemed to come and go frequently. The facility was a revolving door for any of them. I wanted to be intentional and impactful with them, but I kept thinking there was so much more that I could have done for them. I found it extremely difficult to make an impact in their lives. I wasn't seeing lasting progress for these girls.

I asked the members of our team what they thought we could do to contribute. I desired to see measurable results in the form of impact and change. Collectively we came up with so many excuses for our lack of progress as leaders. We started to blame the youth and their lack of engagement by saying things like "they're too far gone" or "they're not ready."

I saw how the young women started off great and then ended badly. I wanted to learn how to be a better vessel for them. I felt like my life wasn't too different from theirs. I recall one young woman who couldn't seem to get it together. The staff warned her that if she came back she was going to have to go to a far more restrictive facility, but it didn't matter because she returned. People were struggling to do better. I wondered why my story wasn't connecting to their story in a way that would cause them to turn the page to do something better. So I began to brainstorm ways to accomplish that.

My true purpose began to reveal itself when I volunteered at Nesting Doves. It was a home for unwed mothers. Nesting Doves was a state-run agency where young pregnant women resided until they birthed their babies. The young women were able to receive counsel, and be assisted in making decisions about the fate of their unborn child. They could choose to keep their child after delivery or to place them up for adoption. This ministry became near and dear to my heart. I ran the department and worked with a team of women who came together to develop curriculum, and to help establish a foundation as mentors for the young women.

There were times when I would be required to become the midwife for them when circumstances warranted it. Their parents either lived in Indiana or out of the stay.

Some of the young women's parents disowned them altogether. I witnessed some disheartened situations. Some of the girls were as young as eleven years old. My life was impacted when I was present during the time a twelve-year-old girl delivered her baby. I supported her in the absence of her mother, but my presence wasn't enough. In her pain, she screamed constantly for her mother as she delivered her baby. In that moment I realized just how young the girl was, and how scared she must have been.

Things were bad for them. There were rape victims or girls who decided to have sex at an early age. I commended the girls for being courageous enough to have their babies, or for making the decision to place them up for adoption. I could identify with their plight since I had an abortion as a teen.

One of the first curricula I developed for Nesting Doves was called "A Woman's Worth". The basic premise was to allow the young women to get to know themselves. They did this by exploring their own beliefs and values through a series of questions. We answered these questions as a group during a question and answer session. The curriculum was invaluable, and it helped them discover purpose. We met once a week to explore their ideas. Another activity I had encouraged them to participate in community service. I used the church's van to take the young women to the rescue mission to help serve meals or anything else that was needed. It helped them to utilize the cause initiatives model, and to give back since they too were being supported by the state as well. I taught them that no matter how much they felt like they didn't have, there is always enough for others. It was my first opportunity to teach others to move progress forward with their limited beliefs to accomplish much.

CHAPTER 10

Reflection

Life has a funny way of allowing us to experience things that at the time don't seem to add value to our greater purpose. I knew, however, that I was manifesting purpose while participating in several non-profit ventures. Each of these opportunities was different. I wasn't sure of the magnitude to which I'd reap the benefits, but I remained still and in the presence of the God. I knew without a doubt that He was ordering my footsteps. I allowed my servant heart to help the women involved in these projects by allowing them to be the thread that was woven into the better parts of myself. I realized that I was gaining valuable knowledge and skills while still exploring my purpose. I was grateful to be able to work with women from all walks of life, cultures, and ages. Another valuable lesson, "sharpen your saw and fill up your toolkit with invaluable resources that can be utilized for the greater good of others." It's called "protecting your craft to perfect your purpose." I thank God that He kept me motivated, and I had the will to stay afloat even when I felt stagnant, fulfilled, then unfulfilled, elated, then discontented, but He never let me quit. My goal was never to live life with regrets or to live a life without taking risks. In the moment, you have to be intentional at whatever stage you are doing in life. You have to follow the leadings of your passions and desires. Those things will eventually lead to God's purpose for your life.

CHAPTER 11

Planning Fearlessly

There were times in my life as an adult woman where I struggled to embrace my fierceness. I'd looked in the mirror, and the person looking back at me was a version of my younger self. She was the girl who hadn't been supported, the one who had to fight for everything good and bad in her life. I grieved for her and the things she never achieved, but still longed for; however, God had a plan for her, and I'm walking in it with no apologies or regrets.

The first fifteen years of my professional life, I worked diligently to create change for companies. I did this by engaging their employees and helping them to generate purposeful movement. Evidence proved that things were working, but what I did notice most was that the employees seemed to be cooperating out of obligation. I wanted to reach people on a deeper personal level, and to help them buy into the process of change on an individual basis to make their lives better.

I recall thinking that there has to be so much more that I could be doing to help other's cross over the finish line in their own lives. There was a stirring in my spirit, and I wanted more for myself and others. I envisioned a transition place that would help people in need. It would be a program that would offer individualized mentoring or accountability partners to achieve success. I didn't realize that God was already preparing the foundation of such a place for me.

I'll never forget how things began to materialize. I could feel God working on my spirit, and he was healing my wounds so that I could be used for His glory. I had been out in the community running errands when I ran into an old friend. I was taken aback when I noticed that she wasn't as polished and professional as I remembered her to be. I asked her how she was doing, and she told me that she had taken the buy-out at Chrysler where she worked as a Human Resources Director. She said that she was finding it difficult to obtain employment with the compensation she was accustomed to. She told me that she was depressed and floundering. I listened intently as she shared her concerns. Then she said something that I couldn't ignore.

She told me that she just needed "personal accountability." I had never heard anyone use that terminology. They used it to make the point that their life had gotten so off track that they needed someone to partner with to get them on the right track.

I recall having a conversation with my husband afterward, and I told him about my plan. I asked him why Kokomo didn't have grants or funding that could help support women on a case by case basis, to help get assistance with putting their intention on the table. I realized that people were struggling and wanted a model or mentor who could actually show them the ropes of success. My initial thought was for the women to have a case manager or an accountability transition counselor. Coaching was the very thing that I envisioned myself doing, but I never knew what it was called. I prayed for that woman, and asked God if what she shared with me was something I needed to speak, seek, and receive as His will. He answered with a resounding yes!

In that moment, the scripture John 21:6 came to me, where the Lord instructed his disciples to "Cast the net on the right side of the ship, and ye shall find." I began to meditate on His word and to share my desires with others, and things started happening for me. My husband encouraged me to follow my dreams. My close friend and I began considering business options, and she asked if I had even heard of a Life Coach. The terminology was foreign, but she explained the role of a Life Coach and encouraged me to do some research.

After researching, I came across a coaching program that I wanted to pursue at IPEC Coaching out of New Jersey. I followed my plan and did the work to become a Certified Professional Coach, then started my business LCR Coaching shortly thereafter. Working with and empowering women has always been the plan. I infused my power, kickstarted my purpose, and now my plan materialized. I've been able to work with some exceptional women who come from all walks of life and backgrounds. However, the thing I enjoy most is partnering with businesses to help professionals collectively work together to establish a plan. Being able to walk alongside women who want to elevate their leadership potential, while creating a work culture that cultivates team spirit brings me great fulfillment. I don't have to, I get to! I get the opportunity to help them and their employees cross the finish line with success.

I told myself to "stay available and be ready." God is going to call you to create engagement, movement, and change. I had already had an executive seat at the table and knew what it took to make real change happen. I had a well-rounded view about human behavior, change management, and the process of helping people make change by taking things from one state to another. The plan was very simple it had a heartbeat of life purpose. I was able to help people shift internally to commit to something much more meaningful for them. Like becoming an entrepreneur, corporate leader, business manager, team leader, or even the CEO of the company was starting to become very clear to me. Helping women to explore all their options allowed me to be a good steward of my gifts.

I tell women what I've learned "you've always got to have your toolkit ready because you never know when you will have to go back and use those tools, you have to sharpen your tools daily!" For me, it was in speaking, writing, engaging, teaching others, creating curriculum, learning technology, understanding human behavior, implementing change management strategies, serving the community, and pursuing higher education. There were many times along the way that I doubted myself early on. I had to come to grips that God has called me to this place. No matter what happens the plan for my life is essential to complete, and that negative thinking can sabotage this success. Sometimes we drop the ball and don't get it right. At times, we have to get back up and try again. We've got one shot at this race called life, and we might as well live it. If this calling on your life is the real deal, then sitting still is not an option.

After launching LCR Coaching, I gravitated to what seemed to be gravitating towards me. I worked with people in the community men and women, it didn't matter. I agreed to help them figure their lives out. I was just getting started, so I had to build my business from scratch while sharpening my tools. I created all of the branding material that you see for my business. I developed my own website and had three by the time I was done. I was exploring with each client what worked and what didn't. This helped me put my plan together. After doing my research and working with clients that allowed me to learn from them, I reintroduced myself to the community as an entrepreneur. I learned at that moment we don't have to ask anyone's permission or obtain someone else's validation to live connected to the values that matter to us. We are obligated to stay true to our core values, and I don't get any do-overs in this life.

In life, we are always looking for others to validate our plan instead of taking action. I had an overwhelming feeling of grief when I was almost finished with my coaching certification. I couldn't believe that everything I had done in my life was part of my business plan. The reason for my sadness was that I felt that I should have obtained my certification years ago in my twenties. Where was this at? Why didn't I know about this sooner? I was finally doing what I loved to do.

I believed that I had a lot of making up to do and ground to cover. I had to start trusting myself and what I was called to do. I wanted to create opportunities for people to obtain the progress and growth that they needed to experience personally and professionally. I researched and learned everything I could to figure out what ignites the plan in people, and concluded that it's when a person's power, purpose, and plan is infused. It was happening for me, and my desire to help others get there's was too.

Before igniting the plan in people and not too long after I started LCR Coaching I went to Indianapolis to Capelli

Salon Studios to get my hair done. 106.7 WTLC radio which is a popular African American station was broadcasting live in the studio. The station was sponsoring a Women Empowerment Conference hosted by Karen Vaughn. During their live show on the radio in the salon, they were encouraging people to get their tickets to the conference. At this point in my business, I was always looking for opportunities to get it out in the community. Karen Vaughn just happened to come up to me to share the flyer to the event and encouraged me to come. I immediately responded by inquiring about vendor opportunities. Karen asked what it was I did, and I told her that I was a Start-Up Business Coach. She said that she was looking for a business coach and wanted to know what I would teach on within forty-five minutes if given the opportunity. I instantly went into pro-mode, and I knew right then and there that God had given me my moment. I was at the right place at the right time. I pulled out my toolkit because you always have to be ready. I gave Karen my elevator speech, and I knew what she was asking of me and I was prepared. She invited me to write down what I could provide entrepreneurs by sending her a proposal. I gave her my business card that I designed myself and still use today. I couldn't wait to leave the salon to get home to prepare the proposal she requested. I realized that I had one shot and this was it.

I put together an amazing outline and named it "Make Your Side Hustle Your Main Hustle." It was perfect, I got a call the very next day. Karen asked me to be the second guest speaker at the event that would be held at the Indiana Farmer's Coliseum. She asked me to be a subject matter expert on content that I had developed over a lifetime. When I arrived at the event, I had a million-dollar attitude. I wore a white power suit, but for a minute I lost my confidence and thought that no one was going to show up for me. The gremlin in my head was trying to destroy the day God had planned for me. My notes on my computer wouldn't load, I didn't have access to the internet to open the notes I sent myself through email. I was surely about to pass out, this was surely not happening. In that moment people started to pile in, more than what I mentally imagined. First, I was afraid no one would show, and now I'm nervous because there is a crowd of people and I have no notes. My family had to assure me that I'd do great. Needless to say, I rocked it. I asked the DJ to play a Mary Mary song called "Go get it," and I was on fire.

Everything I prepared for was ingrained in me, and it didn't matter that I didn't have my notes. Everything I experienced as a teenager developed my voice and being a Christian helped it all merge together. There was a collage of things that I wanted to say to the women in the audience. I was a roaring lion who laid it all on the line. I didn't know who was there, but what I did know was that I was offering an open call for women to take action in their own lives. I was allowing them to receive two free hours of coaching with me. Nearly one hundred women accepted the call. It was a long several months of coaching for me, but it was worth it. Karen Vaughn propelled me forward by offering me a bigger seat at the table to help women.

Business is picking up, and I increased my credibility when I partnered with the local radio station. I was considered a subject matter expert on business coaching. It was all a part of the plan and I was able to grow, learn, and continue to sharpen my saw. I was learning all I could about maximizing by exposure to attract new business opportunities. I utilized search engine optimization better known as SEO for my website. It didn't take long to start getting hits for Business Coaching opportunities. I recall being on vacation, around New Year's one year. I checked my website not expecting anything and received a hit for a Business Coaching opportunity. I was so happy, all my hard work and time I invested into my business was paying off.

I opened the email, and it read, "This is my situation, this is what I need and what can you do to help," I couldn't believe it. In that moment all my experience in different aspects of coaching came to the forefront. Everything I had learned while sitting in an executive seat with the government agency is now coming into play now. I didn't hesitate to contact the owner of the email. I was given an extensive interview. I was asked several questions especially about how I felt about the DISC personality and the Myers Brigs personality test. She was interested in my thoughts about business overall and wanted to know more. I gave her my honest opinion and told her that instead of analyzing personalities, I would rather know why an employee behaves a certain way. Needless to say, she hired me.

I began attracting multiple employers who needed a Business Coach to come in and help turn things around. My philosophy was "If I can get to the head then I can help the feet." It's not uncommon for the head to be oblivious to the pain their workers are in; therefore, real change can't happen. Others continued to inquire and invest into my services, and as I advocated for helping people I kept moving forward. My net widened as I continued to move ahead to pursue additional opportunities. I also made a point to contribute ten percent of my coaching practice to charitable giving. So I could help assist individuals that might not have the resources to invest in themselves. I want to be able to be a good steward to people that God said I need to work with regardless of their financial status. It goes back to day one. Everything I've done has been for the elevation of women so that they would have a voice. Thus, The Women's Power Brunch was birthed in 2016.

CHAPTER 11

Reflections

Reflection: The Gifts God gave me are a dream come true, and I experienced them through my powerful experiences. The fortitude it took to navigate through life back then was something other's may have seen as too difficult and may have thrown in the towel, but I refused to give up. I was able to find my voice, and it allowed me to speak boldly and loud for others who hadn't found theirs. My power was infused with purpose which I solely received through being a Christian and having a personal relationship with my Lord and Savior, Jesus Christ. It was He who help me through various life experiences to find my purpose. My life purpose metaphor is "I am the Ray that causes a deep breath that awakens the soul." This knowing wasn't just for me, but for others who I have personal influence. My husband Vaughn has partnered with me throughout most of this incredible journey to encourage me whenever I couldn't see the end of the rainbow. God has a funny sense of humor, he laughs when we think we have it all figured out about who's the one or who's 'not' the one. Vaughn has been my perfect gift, and I thank God for him daily. My children and now my grandchildren are those glimmers of hope and rays of light that infuse me with new power, and they give me permission to dream bigger dreams. #PowerPurposePlan is not some little catchy phase, it's a movement that I stand behind. It's the vehicle that will continue to allow me to help women which was God's plan all along.

THE PLAN

The City of Firsts
United State of Women Power Brunch

Kalena James is the founder of LRC Coaching. She decided to host the City of Firsts United State of Women Power Brunch in 2016. This purpose of this exciting event was to host a VIP experience that joins together female socialites, inspirational leaders, business moguls, and powerhouse influencers for an afternoon of enrichment. As an opportunity to partake in a delicious brunch and to network, be inspired, and receive an up-close personal experience to obtain a wealth of wisdom from some elite women who are equipped to sow into their power, purpose, and plan! Her mission is to rally women together to celebrate what we have achieved personally and professional, generate opportunities to bond with like-minded women and inspire changemakers to create action in their communities and the world. This is a movement! Leadership development in the areas of Increasing Women's Economic Empowerment, Violence Against Women, Advancing Women Entrepreneurship & Innovation, Women's Health, Wellness & Work Balance, and Leadership & Civil Engagement are the priorities.

The United State of Women was birthed from the heartbeat of our very own White House. Run by our Civil Nation. THE UNITED STATE OF WOMEN gives a megaphone to the importance of women equality and provides a platform for topics that are important to women. Though LCR Coaching can't speak on behalf of the Civic Nation, LCR Coaching aligns itself with its mission to educate and elevate leadership talent. Find us on Facebook #powerpurposeplan or http://uswkokomo.com

http://www.theunitedstateofwomen.org

THE PLAN

The Bridge Academy

Wonderful benefits are possible for every woman in "The Bridge Academy," LCR Coaching is providing women the opportunity to tap into professional support and leadership training they may not have been able to capture on their own.

Ladies, if you are looking for a chance to build your business and Leadership strengths; this is a bridge to do so. The Bridge will help women leverage their ability to prosper successfully through interactive learning sessions and connect you with thought leaders who are experts in their field who will partner with you when you need individual support.

The Mission:

- Educate and advance women's personal and professional leadership skills
- Provide cutting edge, thought-provoking training content and exceptional learning experiences for women
- Enables women to surround themselves with people who are equipped to help them succeed
- offer women a mentor, coach or accountability partner when needed

The Bridge Academy birthed in 2017, from the heartbeat of the Power Brunch mission – "Help educate and elevate leadership potential," will be fully operational in the spring of 2018. The one and two-day in-person sessions, seminars, workshops or one-hour conference calls will provide women a safe and ingenious platform to explore their Power- Purpose-Plan. The Bridge Academy connects women to professionals who are subject matter experts in their field, provide real-time learning from real-world experiences, and provides individual backing when they want it.

Our Preferred Speaker are the best in their field. Our network consists of women:

- Executives
- Managers
- Supervisors
- Professional women in a leadership role
- Women business owners
- Certified professional coaches
- Medical professionals
- Certified therapist and counselors
- Community leaders
- Successful entrepreneurs

Our preferred speakers are noteworthy experts who are available and ready to help women take that leap to the next level. You can't go wrong with partners who can be an accountability partner, consultant, coach, trainer, and teacher.

You name it; the Bridge Academy has it. The benefit of participation is to help women cross over to overcome obstacles that are often stagnant to their growth. The Bridge Academy offers not only in-person workshops but also real-time conference calls where women can take an hour out of their busy day to gain information that can be applied instantly.

Experts in their respective platforms are professional all over the world and right here in our Kokomo community. As the Academy grows, we are looking for gifted women who can help develop other women who utilize our services. The benefit of being a Preferred Speaker in the Bridge Academy is two-fold, it will provide opportunities to connect to women who can benefit from their expertise and services, and an opportunity to surround themselves with leaders and like-minded professionals who are paving the way for others. Behind the scene, Preferred Speakers will take part in exclusive retreats for personal development. LRC Coaching is always looking and welcomes talented women with vision who are willing to assist other women. If you have the heart to serve and are looking for leadership opportunities to grow others contact us by email kalenajames@lcrcoaching.com or visit us at http://LCRCoaching.com/thebridge.

www.ingramcontent.com/pod-product-compliance
Lightning Source LLC
Chambersburg PA
CBHW032112090426
42743CB00007B/330